MAKE, STITCH
& KNIT FOR BABY

An Hachette UK Company
www.hachette.co.uk

First published in the UK in 2020 by Ilex,
an imprint of Octopus Publishing Group Ltd
Carmelite House
50 Victoria Embankment
London EC4Y 0DZ
www.octopusbooks.co.uk
www.octopusbooksusa.com

Published in France by
Hachette Livre
58, rue Jean-Bleuzen,
92170 Vanves

Photography and styling: Émilie Guelpa
Artistic direction: Émilie Guelpa
Design: Frédéric Voison
Adaptation: Dominique Montembault

Copyright © Hachette Livre (Marabout) 2020
Published by arrangement with Hachette Livre.
First published in France in 2018.

Distributed in the US by
Hachette Book Group
1290 Avenue of the Americas
4th and 5th Floors
New York, NY 10104

Distributed in Canada by
Canadian Manda Group
664 Annette St.
Toronto, Ontario, Canada M6S 2C8

Publisher: Alison Starling
Editorial Director: Zena Alkayat
Managing Editor: Rachel Silverlight
Editor: Jenny Dye
Editorial Assistant: Ellen Sandford O'Neill
Translator: Simon Jones, assisted by Wendy Morris
Art Director: Ben Gardiner
Page layout: Tammy Kerr
Production Controller: Lisa Pinnell

ISBN 978-1-78157-760-8

A CIP catalogue record for this book is available
from the British Library.

Printed and bound in China

10 9 8 7 6 5 4 3 2 1

Disclaimer
Every effort has been made to ensure that all the
information in this book is accurate. However, due
to differing conditions, tools and individual skills,
the publisher cannot be responsible for any injuries,
losses and other damages that may result from the
use of the information in this book.
All reasonable care has been taken to recommend
the safest methods of working for the craft projects
in this book. Before starting any task, you should be
confident that you know what you are doing, and
that you know how to use all the tools, equipment
and materials safely. You must always use such
items with care and follow the manufacturer's
instructions. Neither the author nor the publishers
can accept any legal responsibility or liability for
any direct or indirect consequences arising from
this book or the information contained within.

MAKE, STITCH & KNIT FOR BABY

35 SUPER-CUTE AND EASY CRAFT PROJECTS

ÉMILIE GUELPA

When I was pregnant with my daughter Louise, I began to think about how I would decorate her bedroom. I realized that there were so many things to do and so many possibilities – I began to imagine the beautiful colours, materials and textures that I could work with. As an expectant mother, it was a new space for unlimited creativity, inspiration and focus.

Then, once Louise had arrived and as the weeks went by, I began to learn her likes and dislikes, and I wanted to create things to awaken her senses and to allow them to gently develop at her own pace. I wanted her environment to be full of happiness and things made with love.

In this book I have aimed to show a variety of projects inspired first by my pregnancy, and then by my daughter and her babyhood. I've included the things she enjoyed discovering, touching, playing with, and things I have enjoyed making for her, which will, I hope, stay with her for many years. I wanted to retain the memory of this first year spent with her, before she grew too big!

Whether you are expecting a baby, are already a mum or a dad, or you simply want to make something special for someone who is awaiting the arrival of their child, I – we – sincerely hope that this book will inspire your creativity and your desire to make lovely things.

This book is all the more dear to my heart because it is the work of three pairs of hands: mine, those of Louise, who posed for the book, and also those of my Mum, who sewed with me for many long weeks using my grandmother's sewing machine. Three – almost four – generations of women together! Each of us put into it this positive energy that will, I hope, touch you as much as it has helped us to make this book. Happy reading.

Émilie, Élisabeth and Louise

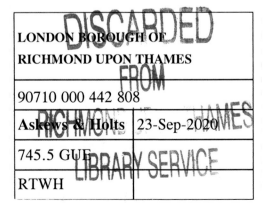
Find me on **WWW.GRIOTTES.FR**

CONTENTS

ON THE GO / 88

TO PLAY / 106

FOR BEDTIME / 156

TOOL BOX

For this book I have used many different techniques, tools and materials to suit the desires of everyone. Some tools crop up time and again though, so here is a far from exhaustive list:

• A magic embroidery pen. This is a must-have. It has enabled me to do embroidery very easily – although, if you are a confident embroiderer and prefer to use a traditional embroidery needle, there is no need to buy an embroidery pen.

• In the same vein, its big sister, the punch needle, will allow you to embroider thicker wool (and tapestry wool). Various sizes are available, and you can choose a size to suit the type of yarn you are using.

• Pompoms, felt balls, wooden beads of all sizes – round or hexagonal – good-quality dressmaking scissors, different kinds of fabric, a sewing machine (but fear not – you don't need to be an expert to create the very simple projects in this book), gold thread, sequinned elastic ribbon, and more.

• A whole range of stranded cotton threads for embroidery, a glue gun, thin and thick felt, coloured paper, tracing paper for transferring patterns, and more…

In short, simple tools – but essential ones!

Have fun!

WARNING

For obvious safety reasons, you must supervise your child properly when they are playing with an object. Carefully check that all elements of your handmade creations are sound and firmly attached, especially if they contain small parts. Never leave your child alone with a toy.

This book features predominantly decorative items, which are not meant to be used by a baby but rather to decorate their bedroom and surroundings.

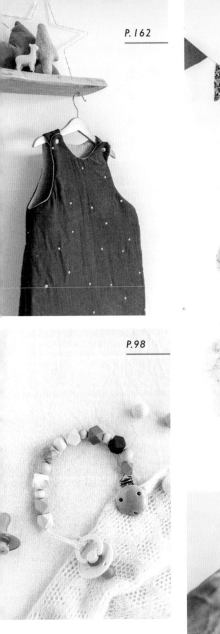

P. 162

P. 40

P. 30

P. 136

P. 98

P. 62

P. 83

P. 158

P. 114

P. 176

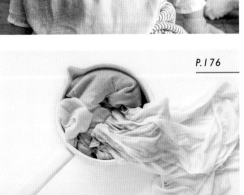

TO DECORATE

STEP 1.

STEP 2.

STEP 3.

MATERIALS & METHOD

EMBROIDERED CUSHION

45 X 25 CM (18 X 10 IN) FLORAL FABRIC
45 X 25 CM (18 X 10 IN) DOUBLE GAUZE
GOLD EMBROIDERY THREAD
SEWING THREAD TO MATCH THE FABRIC
TRACING PAPER
PENCIL
AIR- OR WATER-ERASABLE FABRIC MARKER
PEN (OPTIONAL)
EMBROIDERY HOOP
MAGIC EMBROIDERY PEN
SHORT LENGTH OF THIN WIRE
FABRIC SCISSORS
SEWING NEEDLE OR SEWING MACHINE
HOLLOWFIBRE STUFFING

Cushions are really easy projects to get started with, and this one allows you to practise your embroidery skills, too. You could add the baby's name or date of birth, and experiment with different fabrics and thread colours.

1. Using the templates on page 183, trace the letters or numbers you need to form the baby's name or date of birth, then transfer them to the floral fabric using a pencil or erasable fabric marker pen (see page 180; you can buy air- or water-erasable fabric marker pens from craft shops or online).

2. Stretch the floral fabric over the embroidery hoop. Don't worry if the word to be embroidered is too large to fit inside the hoop, as you can always move the hoop along later.

3. Using the magic embroidery pen, embroider the outline of the name or date, and then fill it in to produce a good thickness (see page 24 for how to thread an embroidery pen using the short length of thin wire and pages 120–1 for the technique). If you're a confident embroiderer, you could use a conventional embroidery needle and chain stitch rather than the embroidery pen.

4. Assemble and stuff the cushion following steps 2–4 on page 19, with the flower-patterned fabric on the front and the double gauze on the back.

MATERIALS & METHOD

TASSELLED CUSHION

18 X 32 CM (7 X 12½ IN) LINEN FABRIC
18 X 32 CM (7 X 12½ IN) SILK FABRIC
4 TASSELS MADE FROM SILK THREAD
SEWING THREAD TO MATCH THE TASSELS AND FABRICS
HOLLOWFIBRE STUFFING
PINS
SEWING NEEDLE
SEWING MACHINE (OPTIONAL)

Tassels add a playful and colourful finishing touch to a plain
cushion and the soft texture of the silk is perfect for little hands
to explore. Make sure the tassels are sewn on really firmly.

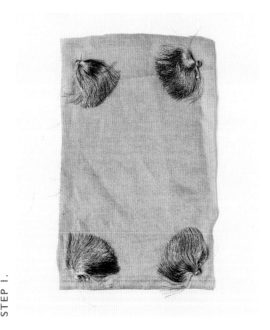

STEP 1.

Lay the linen fabric flat, right side up, and place a tassel at each corner, about 1 cm (⅜ in) from the edge of the fabric. Sew the tassels on by hand, making sure they're firmly attached to the fabric.

STEP 2.

Place the silk fabric on top, right sides together. Stitch around by hand (using backstitch) or by machine, 0.5 cm (¼ in) from the edge. Take care not to catch the tassels in the seam. Leave an 8–10-cm (3–4-in) gap in one side for the stuffing.

STEP 3.

Turn the cushion right side out. If necessary, re-sew the tassels to make sure they are really secure.

STEP 4.

Stuff the cushion evenly, making sure you push the stuffing right into the corners. Turn the edges of the opening under and slipstitch the opening closed by hand.

FLUFFY CLOUD MOBILE

WHITE WOOL TOPS OR ROVING
GOLD SPARKLY PAPER
WHITE COTTON THREAD
FOAM BLOCK
FELTING NEEDLE
PAPER
PENCIL
SCISSORS
GLUE STICK
SEWING NEEDLE

This mobile would look amazing suspended from a ceiling or shelf! Make a whole series of clouds with different motifs underneath them – perhaps little gold crescent moons in place of the stars or strings of silver sequins for sparkling showers of rain.

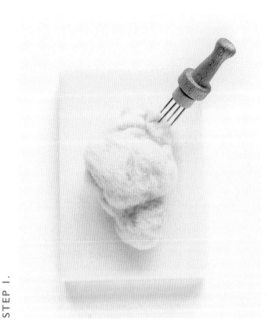

Place the wool tops or roving on the foam block, form it into a rough cloud shape with your fingers, and pierce the wool repeatedly with the felting needle until the wool forms a dense mass. Work slowly and keep your fingers well out of the way of the needle tips.

Photocopy and cut out the stars on page 190. Draw around them onto the the gold paper and cut out to make six stars. Cut three lengths of white cotton thread. Glue the stars together in pairs, with the gold sides facing out and the end of a length of cotton thread sandwiched in the middle.

Thread the other end of the thread through the eye of a sewing needle. Push the needle through the cloud and out the other side. Remove the needle, tie a knot, and cut off the excess thread. Repeat with the other two stars, hanging them at different heights.

Thread the needle with a longer length of cotton and tie the end in a knot. Pass the needle through the middle of the cloud: the knot will catch at the base. Use the excess thread to hang the cloud up from a hook or a pin.

MATERIALS & METHOD

TEDDY BEAR
WALL HANGING

15 X 15 CM (6 X 6 IN) WHITE COTTON FABRIC, PLUS
10 X 10 CM (4 X 4 IN) TO BACK THE EMBROIDERY
14 X 14 CM (5½ X 5½ IN) FUSIBLE BONDING WEB
EMBROIDERY THREADS IN DIFFERENT COLOURS
GOLD EMBROIDERY THREAD
SEWING THREAD TO MATCH THE FABRIC
13-CM (5-IN) EMBROIDERY HOOP
TRACING PAPER
PENCIL
WATER- OR AIR-ERASABLE FABRIC MARKER
PEN (OPTIONAL)
FABRIC SCISSORS
SHORT LENGTH OF THIN WIRE
MAGIC EMBROIDERY PEN
IRON
SEWING NEEDLE

What better way to frame an embroidery than to use the hoop
you stitched it in. This cheerful little teddy will watch over
your little one while they sleep and be a friendly face for them
to wake up to.

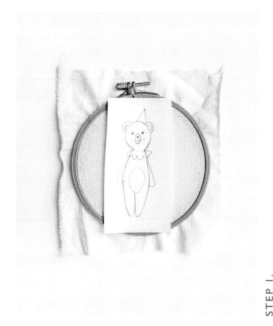

Photocopy the motif on page 201, then transfer it onto the fabric (see page 180). Stretch the cotton fabric over the hoop.

Cut a length of thin wire and make a loop at one end.

Choose the embroidery threads you want to use. You will need around ten different colours.

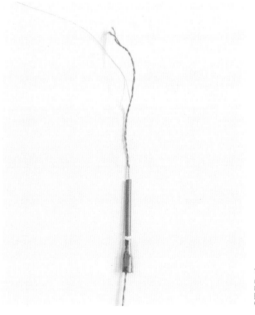

Thread the thin wire through the magic embroidery pen, leaving the loop protruding from its base. Thread brown embroidery thread through the loop and pull the wire to pull the embroidery thread through the eye of the needle.

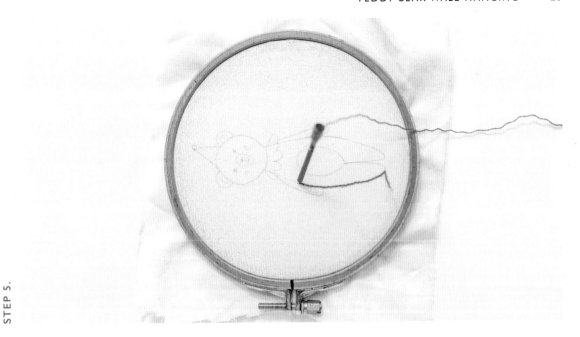

Using the brown thread, embroider the outline of the bear's body and its hind paws on the right side of the fabric (see pages 120–1 for the technique). This gives you flat stitches on the right side of the fabric and looped ones on the reverse.

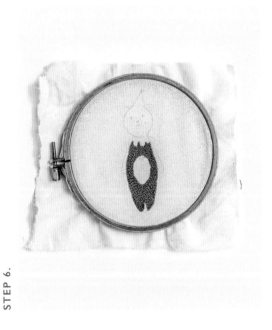

Working from the outside towards the inside, embroider the whole body, with the exception of the bear's tummy.

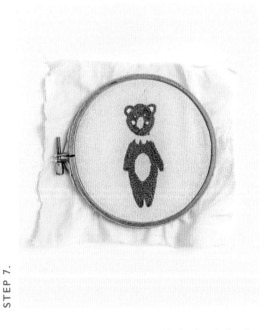

Embroider the front paws and the head, leaving spaces for the inside of the ears, the eyes, the nose and the cheeks.

STEP 8.

STEP 9.

Still working on the right side, using the black thread, make small flat stitches for the eyes, nose and mouth.

Turn the hoop over and embroider the tummy with ecru thread on the back of the fabric. This will produce a more textured, looped stitch on the front of the fabric when you turn it back over.

STEP 10.

STEP 11.

Still working on the back of the fabric, embroider the inside of the ears and the cheeks in pink thread, and the hat in yellow.

To embroider the ruff, sew small stitches in gold thread on the back of the fabric, across the whole width of the ruff. As you sew these stitches, pull on the loops of thread on the front of the fabric to produce long loops.

Turn the hoop back over, so the front is facing you. Embroider small coloured circles and rectangles all around the bear, using different-coloured threads. Add a couple of small pink or red stitches to create a 'pompom' on the top of the bear's hat. Remove the fabric from the hoop. Following the manufacturer's instructions, cut a piece of fusible bonding web big enough to cover the back of the embroidery and use an iron to fuse it in place.

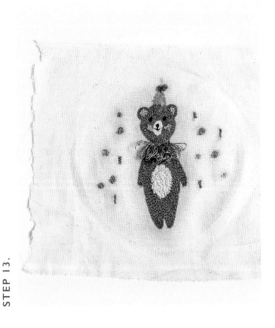

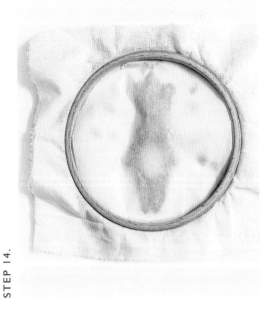

Cut a piece of white cotton fabric the same size as the fusible web. Peel off the backing paper from the fusible web. Place the cotton fabric on top, cover with a tea towel and carefully fuse in place with your iron. Stretch the embroidery over the hoop, with the screw at the top of the design.

Cut off the excess fabric, leaving just enough to fold over the inner hoop. Using the sewing needle and thread, sew a running stitch around the hoop in the excess material. Pull the thread to gather the fabric at the back, and tie a knot to secure.

MATERIALS & METHOD

PUNCH NEEDLE CUSHION

40 X 80 CM (16 X 32 IN) FABRIC SUITABLE FOR PUNCH NEEDLE
WOOL IN DIFFERENT COLOURS
SEWING THREAD TO MATCH THE FABRIC
HOLLOWFIBRE STUFFING
LARGE WOODEN PHOTO FRAME OR EMBROIDERY FRAME
DRAWING PINS AND STAPLER (IF USING A PHOTO FRAME)
PENCIL OR WATER- OR AIR-ERASABLE FABRIC MARKER PEN
PUNCH NEEDLE
FABRIC SCISSORS
SEWING NEEDLE OR SEWING MACHINE

This tactile cushion uses the punch-needle technique to create eye-catching, geometric shapes of brightly coloured wool. By alternating between stitching on the front and the back of the fabric, you can create two very different textures for your baby to explore.

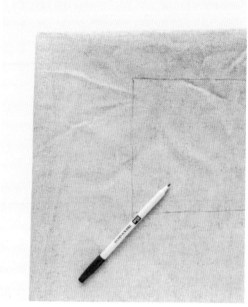

If you are using a photo frame, stretch the punch needle fabric over the frame and pin or staple it to the back. Alternatively, use a large square embroidery frame.

Use a pencil or erasable fabric marker pen to draw the shapes from page 199 onto the fabric, taking care to do this in the lower part of the frame – the top part will fold over to form the back of the cushion.

Choose the wools you want to use. You will need around ten different colours. As you will not be using much of each colour, you could also make use of any leftover ball ends.

STEP 4.

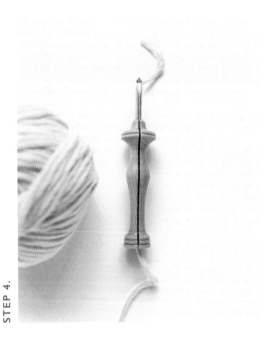

Thread the first colour you want to use into the punch needle (see pages 118–19).

STEP 5.

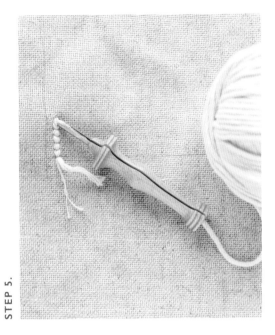

Starting with a corner, begin embroidering on the front of the fabric (see pages 120–1). Work the outline of the shape first and then fill it in, working from the outside inwards.

STEP 6.

Change to a different colour of wool. Embroider the next shape on the back of the fabric to create a different texture. This will produce small loops on the front side of the fabric.

STEP 7.

Continue in the same fashion, embroidering all the geometric shapes using different colours of wool, and alternating between embroidering on the front and the back of the fabric.

The completed embroidery has coloured geometric shapes that all look and feel very different.

Remove the embroidery from the frame.

Trim the edges of the fabric, leaving an even margin around the embroidery. Fold the top part of the fabric over the embroidery, right sides together, so that what will be the front and back of the cushion are facing each other.

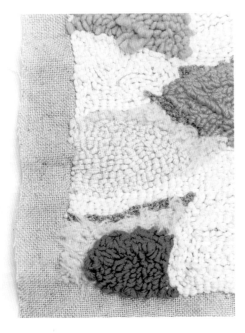

Sew all around the embroidery by hand (using backstitch) or machine, stitching as close as possible to the embroidery and leaving an opening in one side for the stuffing.

Turn the cushion right side out and fill it with the hollowfibre filling. Slipstitch the opening shut by hand.

MATERIALS & METHOD

WOVEN WALL HANGING

COTTON THREAD
OFF-WHITE WOOL TOPS OR ROVING
THICK LINEN TWINE
A FEW LENGTHS OF CREAM REGULAR SPUN WOOL
WOODEN STICK
WEAVING LOOM
WEAVING NEEDLE
SCISSORS

The soft, snuggly texture of the weaving in this wall hanging is particularly suitable for a baby's room. Using only organic materials – undyed wool, linen and wood – this version has an off-white and cream colour palette, but pastel hues such as powder blue, candy pink or a pale lemon yellow would work just as well.

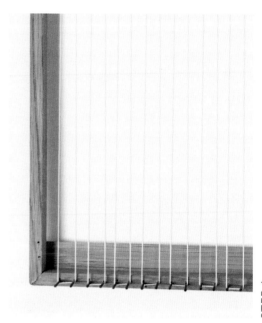

STEP 1.

To warp the loom, tie the cotton thread around the peg in the top left corner. Bring this thread down to the bottom corner and pass it over the first and second pegs on the bottom row, and then back up to the next pegs along on the top row. Repeat this all the way along, so the warp has gaps of two pegs, as in the photo above.

STEP 2.

STEP 3.

Working from left to right, weave in the wool tops with your fingers at the top of the loom. Pass it over two threads, then pull it out to the left between the two threads underneath.

Pass the wool tops over the next two threads, pull it out to the left between the two threads. Pull on it a little – but not too tightly.

STEP 4.

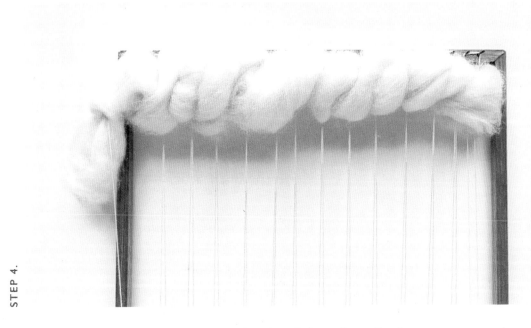

Weave the wool tops to the end of the row, and gently push the wool up to line the woven row up evenly.

STEP 5.

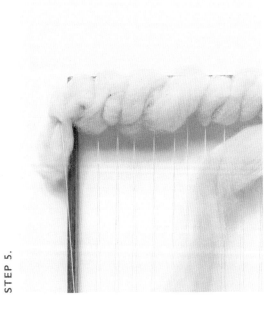

To go back the other way, thread the wool tops around the last warp thread and pull it out between the first two threads on the right.

STEP 6.

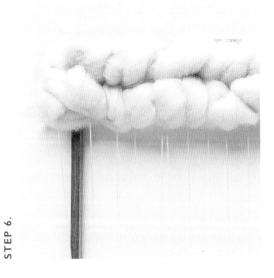

Weave from right to left, passing the wool tops over two threads and pulling it out below and to the right, between the two threads.

Weave eight rows, tightening the rows regularly with your hand.

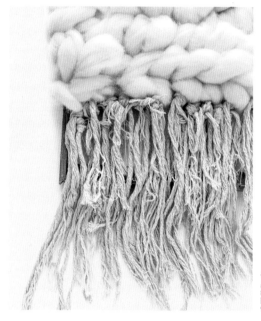

Cut some 20-cm (8-in) lengths of linen twine and fray them slightly with your hands. Tie the twine to two warp threads, directly underneath the woven section, to form a fringe.

Tie twine all along the length of the loom. Add more lengths of twine to the fringe if it is not thick enough.

Lift up the twine and weave five or six rows of regular wool, threading it alternately over and under the warp threads, using a weaving needle. These rows of weaving will reinforce the piece.

Cut the warp threads at the bottom of the loom and tie them together in pairs.

Remove the weaving from the loom by lifting the top threads off the pegs. Slide a wooden stick between the top threads.

STEP 1.

STEP 2.

STEP 3.

MATERIALS & METHOD

BUNTING

PIECES OF DIFFERENT FABRICS
THICK COTTON THREAD OR STRING
PAPER
PENCIL
PINS
PAPER AND FABRIC SCISSORS
PINKING SHEARS
FABRIC GLUE

Nothing brightens up a plain wall better than a string of colourful bunting – and this version is super easy, as you don't even need to do any sewing. It's also a great way of using up small scraps of fabric left over from other projects; alternate plain and patterned material to prevent your bunting from looking too busy.

1. Trace the pattern on page 181 onto a piece of paper and cut it out. Pin it to each of the fabrics in turn and cut out with fabric scissors, following the outline of the pattern.

2. Cut the edges of some of the diamonds – or all of them, if you prefer – with the pinking shears.

3. Lay a diamond flat, wrong side up. Place the cotton thread across the middle, leaving a long piece of thread protruding. Spread some glue onto the fabric, then fold it in two, carefully aligning the edges. If the edges have not been pinked and the material frays, fold the edges of the fabric to the wrong side all around the diamond before you apply the glue and fold it in half. Attach all the diamonds to the thread in this way, spacing them evenly and leaving a long length of thread at the end to attach the bunting to the wall.

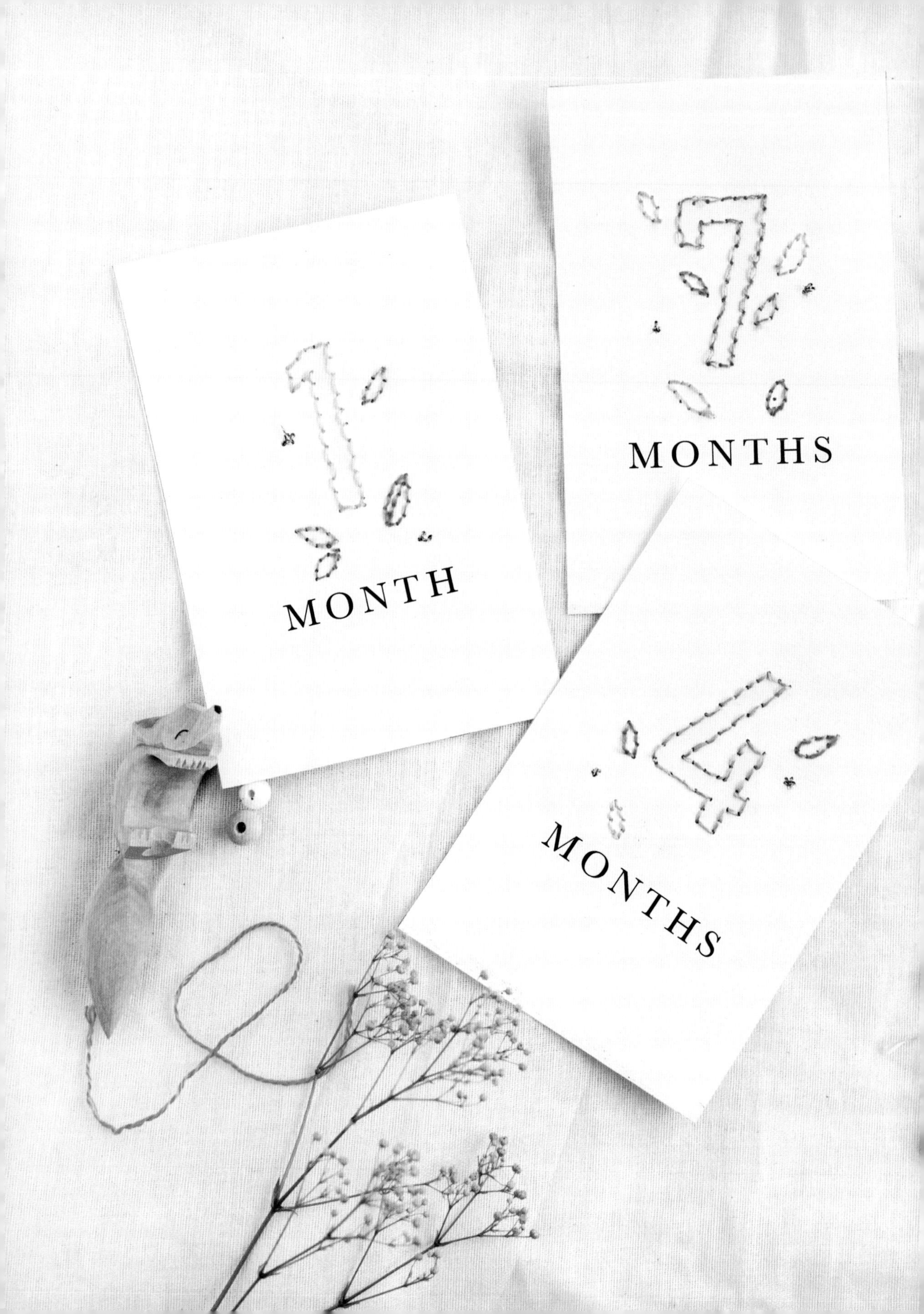
1
MONTH
7
MONTHS
4
MONTHS

MILESTONE CARDS

A4 SHEETS OF THICK DRAWING PAPER
EMBROIDERY THREAD IN PINK, YELLOW, GREEN
AND GOLD
RULER (OPTIONAL)
CRAFT KNIFE (OPTIONAL)
CUTTING MAT OR THICK CARDBOARD (OPTIONAL)
SCISSORS
PAPER OR TRACING PAPER
PENCIL
EMBROIDERY NEEDLE

Babies grow and change so quickly and this project will be a wonderful reminder of those precious first few months. In addition to building up into a treasured photo album for your own little family, it also makes a really special present for doting grandparents.

1. Photocopy the cards on page 182 onto sheets of thick drawing paper, making several copies. Cut them out on a cutting mat or piece of thick cardboard using the ruler and craft knife, or use scissors if you prefer.

2. To transfer the numbers on page 183 onto the cards, photocopy them onto paper or trace them onto tracing paper. Tape the photocopy or tracing over a light source (a lightbox, if you have one, or a window), then tape the drawing paper on top. Go over the tracing lines with a pencil. Draw some simple leaf shapes around the numbers with the pencil.

3. Thread the embroidery needle. Embroider the outlines of the numbers and shapes in colours of your choice, using a back stitch. You might find it helpful to pierce the pencilled outlines with a needle before you start embroidering, as this will make it easier to push the needle through and keep your stitches all the same size.

4. Photograph your baby with a card as each month passes.

MATERIALS & METHOD

CAKE TOPPER

PAPER IN DIFFERENT COLOURS
WHITE PAPER
PENCIL
CRAFT KNIFE (OPTIONAL)
CUTTING MAT OR THICK CARDBOARD (OPTIONAL)
SCISSORS
GLUE STICK
WHITE AND BLACK GEL PENS
2 WOODEN SKEWERS
NON-TOXIC CRAFT GLUE OR CLEAR ADHESIVE TAPE

Even if you're not a baker, or you don't have time to make a cake, you can add a personal touch to your little one's birthday with this cute and easy cake topper.

First, photocopy and cut out the shapes on page 184. Draw around them onto coloured paper. Cut out the shapes using a craft knife on a cutting mat or a piece of thick cardboard (or use scissors if you don't feel confident with a craft knife).

Glue the smaller shapes onto the larger ones, using the photograph opposite or the illustrations on page 185 as a guide.

Glue the different elements together, with the number '1' in the centre, then decorate them with small lines or dots using the white gel pen. Use the black gel pen to draw cute little faces on the animals.

When the glue is completely dry, use the non-toxic craft glue or tape to stick the two skewers to the back, leaving a space between them. Place on top of the cake.

TO WEAR

POMPOM BONNET

BALL OF WHITE WOOL
GOLD WOOL
WOOLLEN BONNET
POMPOM MAKER, 9 CM (3½ IN) DIAMETER
SCISSORS
WOOL NEEDLE

Transform an otherwise plain bonnet into a bespoke one by adding a pompom to the top. It's a thrifty gift idea and pompoms are really easy to make, especially if you have a pompom maker. To create an extra special and eye-catching one, add different coloured threads. You can use any colour and combination of wool, but white and gold looks especially pretty.

1. To begin, open both sides of the pompom maker (see an example of a pompom maker on page 51). Start winding the white wool around one side, occasionally making a few turns with the gold wool. When this side is well covered with several layers of wool, close it into the middle and, without cutting the wool, begin winding more wool around the other side of the pompom maker, adding a few turns of gold wool as you go. The more wool you wind around, the denser the pompom will be. When finished, close the second side into the middle so that your pompom maker is shaped like a circle again.

2. Slip the point of the scissors between the two sides of the pompom maker and cut the wool all around the middle. Pass a long length of wool around the middle of the pompom maker, between the two sides, and tie it firmly. Remove the pompom maker. Cut any protruding bits of wool to make the pompom even, but don't cut the long length of wool you used to tie the pompom yet.

3. Using the wool needle, pass one end of the length of wool that closes the pompom through the top of the bonnet and pull it out the other side. Repeat with the other end of wool, spacing it out slightly to balance the position of the pompom. Pull on the threads to pull the pompom tight against the bonnet, and tie them in a knot on the inside.

MATERIALS & METHOD

SOFT SCARF WITH POMPOMS

1–2 BALLS OF WHITE MERINO YARN
GOLD WOOL (OPTIONAL)
1 PAIR OF KNITTING NEEDLES TO SUIT YOUR
CHOSEN YARN
POMPOM MAKER, 3.5 CM (1½ IN) DIAMETER
SCISSORS
WOOL NEEDLE

Merino yarn is wonderfully soft and cosy, so it's the perfect choice for a baby's sensitive skin. This scarf is made using the simplest of all knitting stitches and finished off with a stylish pompom at each end. Alternatively, you could stitch on a ready-made mini pompom trim. This gift is suitable for children who are a bit older – don't give scarves to very young children.

1. To make the scarf, knit a garter-stitch band (all knit stitches) measuring approx. 60 × 10 cm (24 × 4 in). The paper band on your chosen yarn will give you a recommended needle size and tell you roughly how many stitches you need to cast on for a piece that's 10 cm (4 in) wide.

2. Make two pompoms following the instructions on page 49, using a smaller pompom maker (with a diameter of 3.5 cm/1½ in) and gold wool if you would like. The pompoms will each have two threads hanging from them that can be used to attach them to the scarf.

3. Using the wool needle, sew the two hanging threads across the end of the scarf with a running stitch, from the middle to one edge. Pull on the threads to gather the end of the scarf and tie them firmly together. Repeat with the second pompom at the other end of the scarf.

MATERIALS & METHOD

SHEEPSKIN WAISTCOAT

30 X 75 CM (12 X 30 IN) FAUX SHEEPSKIN WITH
IMITATION SUEDE BACKING
SEWING THREAD TO MATCH THE FABRIC
4-CM (1½-IN) LENGTH OF FLAT GOLD ELASTIC
1 WOODEN BUTTON
PAPER
PAPER AND FABRIC SCISSORS
PINS
SEWING NEEDLE
SEWING MACHINE (OPTIONAL)

Just four straight seams are needed for this cute little waistcoat, so even if you've never sewn a garment before, this one is easily achievable. The faux fabric comes ready backed in imitation suede, so you get an expensive-looking 'lining' without any of the hassle. Best of all, the fabric doesn't fray – so you don't even need to worry about finishing the edges.

STEP 1.

STEP 2.

Photocopy the pattern on page 186 at 250% and cut it out. Cut one back and one front piece from the fabric, cutting 1 cm (⅜ in) beyond the edges of the pattern. Flip the front-piece pattern over and cut a second front piece from the fabric.

Pin the back and fronts right sides together. Sew the shoulder and side seams by hand (using backstitch) or by machine, 1 cm (⅜ in) from the edges.

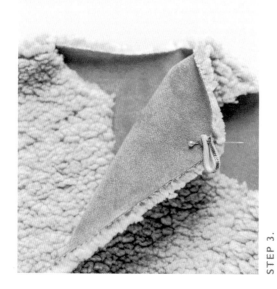

STEP 3.

STEP 4.

Fold the elastic in half and pin both ends to the top of one of the front pieces, on the inside. Hand stitch the ends of the elastic firmly in place.

Sew the wooden button opposite, on the outside of the other front piece.

MATERIALS & METHOD

WAISTCOAT EMBELLISHMENTS

To add a bit more decoration, sew a fringed ribbon down each centre front of the waistcoat, on the right side of the fabric. Personalize your waistcoat by adding ribbons, pompom trims, embroidery, a collar, sleeves or fancy buttons…raid your local haberdashery store and see what takes your fancy!

MATERIALS & METHOD

WARM LITTLE BOOTIES

1 X 100 G (3.5 OZ) BALL OF WHITE DK MERINO YARN
2 LARGE POMPOMS
1 PAIR OF 4-MM (US 6) KNITTING NEEDLES
SCISSORS
WOOL NEEDLE

Just the thing for keeping tiny toes warm and toasty, these cute little booties can be knitted and sewn up in the course of a single evening. This project uses ready-made pompoms to save time, but if you prefer – or if you can't find ready-made ones in a colour you like – you could make your own. Follow the instructions on page 49 and use a small pompom maker about 3.5 cm (1½ in) in diameter.

Following the measurements on page 188, knit two L-shaped pieces in garter stitch (all knit stitches). Then knit two 13 × 6-cm (5 × 2½-in) rectangles.

Lay out one L-shaped piece and one rectangle to form a U-shape as shown above. To join these together using mattress stitch, thread a wool needle with a length of yarn and weave it through a few stitches on the bottom of the L-shaped piece to secure it, bringing the needle out at the bottom right. Push the needle in between the first two rows on the rectangular piece, then in between the first two rows on the L-shaped piece. Continue working upwards in a figure of eight to join the two pieces together. Weave the end of the yarn through the knitting and cut off.

Thread a wool needle with a length of yarn and pass it through the bottom of the U.

Pull on the yarn to gather the bottom. Knot the ends of the yarn and hide them in the stitches.

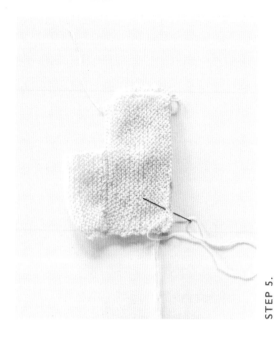

Fold the bootie in half and sew along the entire perimeter.

The bootie will look like this.

Fold the top of the bootie to the inside.

Thread a wool needle with yarn. Push the needle through the front of the bootie, bringing the two sides together.

Pull on the yarn to gather the front of the bootie. Tie it and weave in the yarn ends.

Sew a small pompom onto the bootie. Repeat steps 2–10 to make the other bootie.

MATERIALS & METHOD

BEAUTIFUL BOWS

OFFCUTS OF SOFT, THIN LEATHER AND/OR PIECES
OF STIFF FABRIC, SUCH AS UPHOLSTERY FABRIC
OR THICK COTTON
RIBBON (OPTIONAL)
FABRIC SCISSORS
FABRIC GLUE
STICK-ON CLIP (FOR BOW TIE) OR HOOK-AND-LOOP
TAPE (FOR HEADBAND)

This is a dual-purpose project: it can either be the sweetest little bow tie, with a clip at the back to fasten it to a shirt front, or a headband with the bow as the finishing touch.

1. Decide what you want to make your bow from. You can either use one fabric throughout or a contrasting fabric for the central loop and headband.

2. For each bow, in leather or fabric, cut out a rectangle measuring 10 × 4 cm (4 × 1½ in) and a small, narrow band measuring 4 × 1 cm (1½ × ¼ in).

3. Pinch the rectangle in the middle, roll the narrow band around it, and glue it in place. If you're making a bow tie, glue a clip to the back of the narrow band.

4. For a headband, cut a strip of fabric measuring the circumference of the baby's head plus 3 cm (1¼-in), fold it in half widthways, right sides together, and stitch along the unfolded edge. Turn right side out and press. Alternatively, use a strip of ribbon. Glue the ribbon or fabric strip to the loop of the bow. Glue a 3-cm (1¼-in) long piece of hook-and-loop tape at each end of the ribbon or fabric strip.

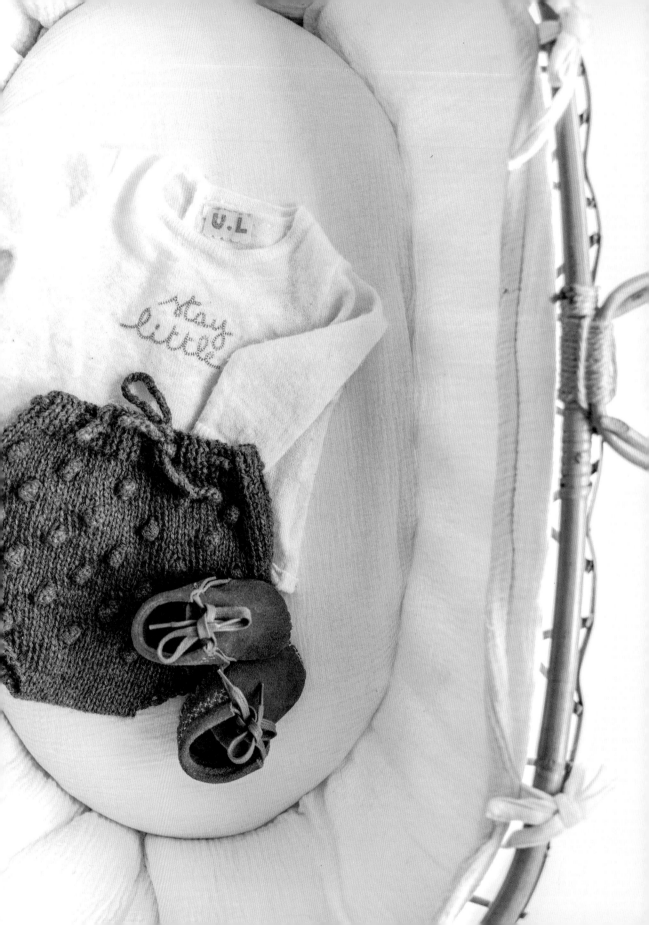

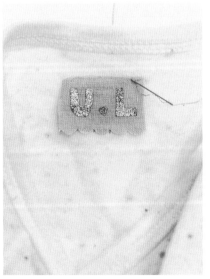

MATERIALS & METHOD

PERSONALIZED NAME TAG

GOLD IRON-ON FABRIC
THICK LINEN FABRIC
GOLD THREAD FOR SEWING
PENCIL
TRACING PAPER
DRESSMAKER'S CARBON PAPER
FABRIC SCISSORS
TEA TOWEL
IRON
SEWING NEEDLE

This is such a quick and easy technique, but it adds a really professional-looking finish to a special garment. You could also use iron-on fabric and the same method to brighten up the front of an inexpensive babygrow or bib with a big, bold shape such as a flower or dinosaur.

1. Using the templates on page 188 and dressmaker's carbon paper, transfer the baby's initials and a small full stop onto the back of the iron-on fabric (see page 180), remembering to reverse the initials, and cut out. Cut out a rectangle, large enough to fit the initals with a border of approximately 1 cm (⅜ in) around them, from the linen fabric.

2. Cut the bottom edge of the linen to produce a scalloped edge. Following the manufacturer's instructions, place the initials and the full stop on the linen and cover with a tea towel. Press with a hot iron to fuse them in place.

3. Backstitch the name tag to the garment using gold thread.

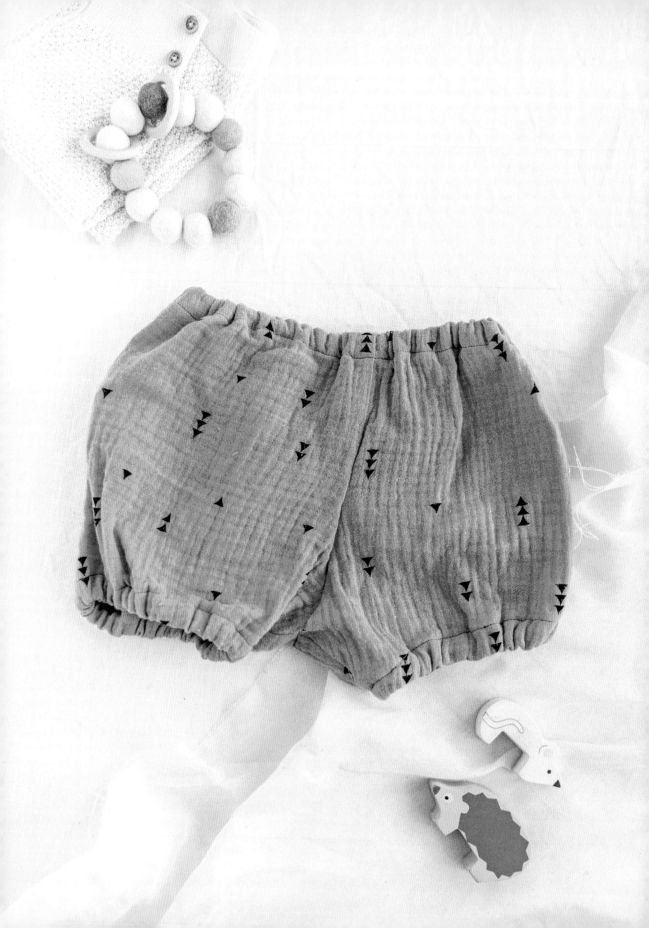

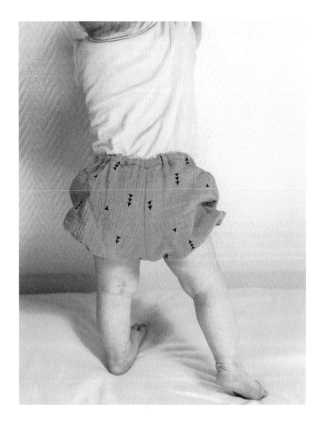

MATERIALS & METHOD

BLOOMERS

70 X 30 CM (28 X 12 IN) COTTON FABRIC
50 CM (20 IN) FLAT ELASTIC, 0.5 CM (¼ IN) WIDE
SEWING THREAD TO MATCH THE FABRIC
PAPER
PAPER AND FABRIC SCISSORS
PINS
SEWING MACHINE
IRON
SAFETY PIN
SEWING NEEDLE

With so many gorgeous printed fabrics on sale, you can create unique garments for your baby that you simply couldn't find on the high street. The elasticated waist and legs on these little bloomers create a snug fit that will keep baby's nappy firmly in place.

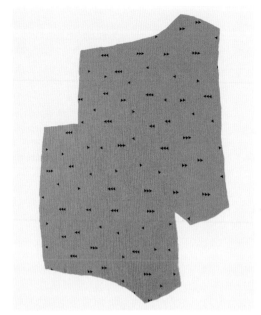

STEP I.

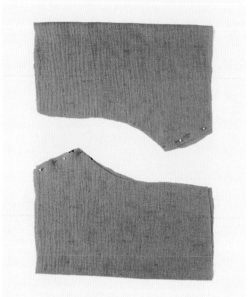

STEP 2.

Photocopy the pattern on page 189, enlarged to 170%, and cut it out. Fold the fabric in half widthways. Pin the pattern pieces to the fabric and cut along the outlines to produce two pieces.

Fold each piece in half, right sides together. Pin as shown in the photo. Sew along the pinned sections, 1 cm (⅜ in) from the edges. Zigzag stitch each side of the seam allowance separately and use the iron to press the seam open.

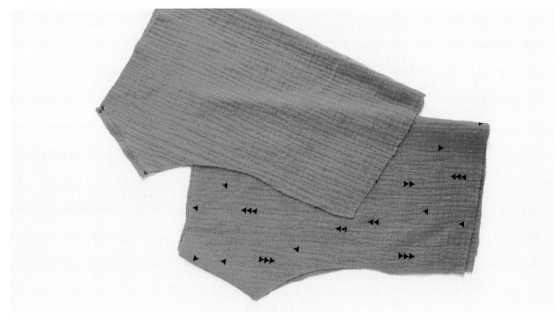

STEP 3.

Turn one of the pieces right side out and slide it into the other.

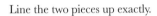

Line the two pieces up exactly.

Pin the two pieces together along the curved edge. Stitch along this curve, 1 cm (⅜ in) from the edge. Zigzag stitch each side of the seam allowance separately to prevent fraying. Press the seam open.

Turn the bloomers right side out.

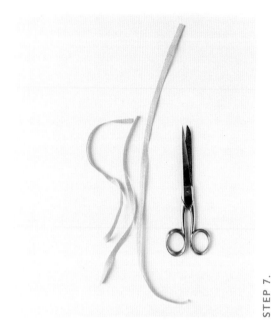

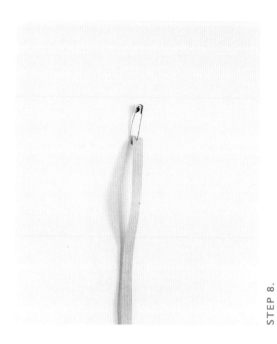

Cut two 15-cm (6-in) lengths of elastic for the legs and one 25-cm (10-in) length for the waist.

Insert a safety pin through one end of the waist elastic.

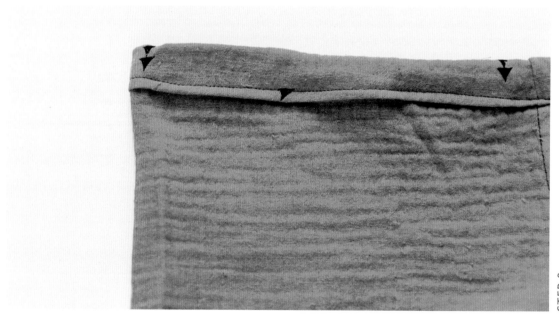

Turn over the waist of the bloomers by 0.5 cm (¼ in) and then 1 cm (⅜ in) and machine stitch all around, leaving a small opening at the back. This creates a casing, or channel, through which you can feed the elastic.

STEP 10.

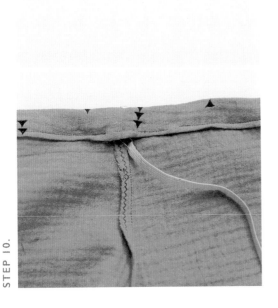

Insert the safety pin into the gap, then use it to feed the elastic all the way round the casing.

STEP 11.

Remove the safety pin, overlap the two ends of the elastic, and sew them together. Push the elastic into the casing.

STEP 12.

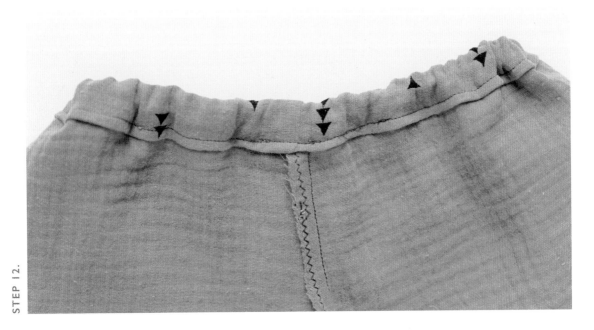

Slipstitch the opening in the casing closed by hand. Fit a length of elastic to the bottom of each leg in the same way.

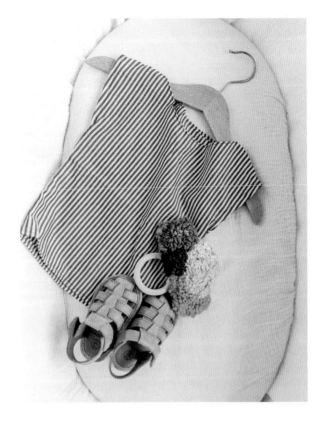

MATERIALS & METHOD

LITTLE SAILOR T-SHIRT

70 X 35 CM (28 X 14 IN) BLUE-AND-WHITE
STRIPED FABRIC
BLUE OR WHITE SEWING THREAD
2 SNAP FASTENERS
PAPER
PAPER AND FABRIC SCISSORS
PINS
SEWING MACHINE AND SEWING NEEDLE

Nautical blue-and-white stripes are perennially popular for both boys and girls and this loose-fitting T-shirt will keep your little one cool on even the hottest of summer days. Use a lightweight woven cotton fabric rather than a jersey knit, as stretch fabrics like jersey are a bit harder to handle if you're new to sewing.

STEP 1.

STEP 2.

Photocopy the pattern on page 187 enlarged to 400% and cut it out. Pin the pattern to the fabric and cut out one front and one back, following the outline of the pattern.

Place the back and front right sides together and pin the shoulders, sides and underarms.

STEP 3.

Starting at the arm holes, sew the shoulder seams 0.5 cm (¼-in) from the edges, but stopping 5 cm (2 in) before the neck. Zigzag stitch the seam allowances. Then sew the side and underarm seams and zigzag stitch the seam allowances.

STEP 4.

STEP 5.

Turn the T-shirt right side out. Turn back 0.5 cm (¼ in), and then another 0.5 cm (¼ in) along the edges of the sleeves and the bottom edge of the T-shirt, and pin.

Hand sew the hems of the sleeves and the bottom of the T-shirt using slipstitch.

STEP 6.

Fold under and pin a 0.5-cm (¼-in) hem on the unstitched 5-cm (2-in) section of the shoulders and around the neck. Hand sew these hems using slipstitch. Attach each side of a snap fastener to each side of one of the shoulders. Repeat with the other shoulder.

MATERIALS & METHOD

FABRIC CROWN

50 X 15 CM (20 X 6 IN) PATTERNED FABRIC
50 X 15 CM (20 X 6 IN) SOFT FABRIC SUCH AS
DOUBLE GAUZE
100 CM (40 IN) GOLD RIBBON, 2 CM (¾ IN) WIDE
SEWING THREAD TO MATCH THE FABRIC
4 SMALL FELT POMPOMS (OPTIONAL)
PAPER
PAPER AND FABRIC SCISSORS
IRON
PINS
SEWING MACHINE (OPTIONAL)
SEWING NEEDLE

Here's an easy-to-make crown for your very own little prince or princess! It's totally reversible, with a jewel-bright patterned fabric on one side and a soft double gauze on the other, so you get two looks in one.

Photocopy the pattern on page 190, enlarging or reducing as necessary so that the bottom edge is the circumference of the child's head plus 1.5 cm (¾ in), to allow for the seams and an overlap. Cut out the pattern. Iron the plain and patterned fabrics to remove any creases. Place the fabrics together and pin the pattern on top. Cut out the fabrics, following the outline of the pattern.

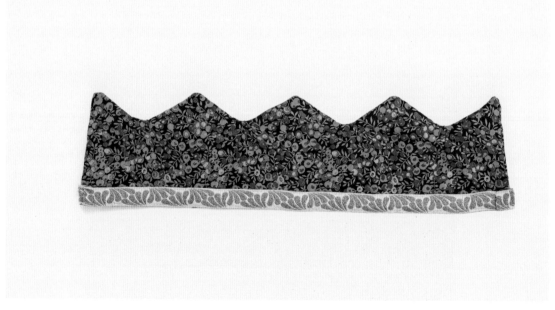

Place the two pieces of fabric right sides together. Sew all around by hand (using backstitch) or by machine 0.5 cm (¼ in) from the edges and and leaving a 10-cm (4-in) opening in the middle of the bottom edge. Turn right side out and press. Turn under the raw edges along the opening and slipstitch the gap closed by hand. Cut the gold ribbon in half. Pin one half to the lower edge of the crown on the patterned side, then trim off any excess ribbon, so it's level with the side edges of the crown. Hand sew the ribbon in place using slipstitch.

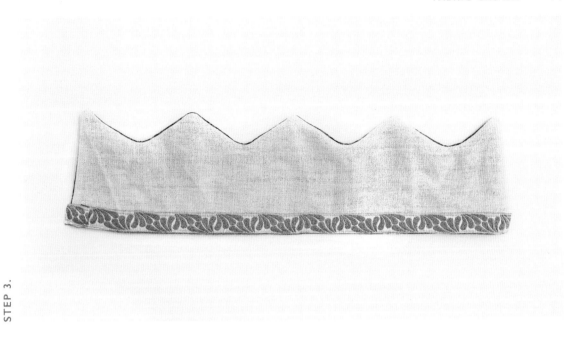

Pin the remaining ribbon to the other side of the crown, trim off any excess and hand sew it on using slipstitch, as before, to make your crown reversible.

Overlap one short end of the crown over the other by 0.5 cm (¼ in) and pin. Hand stitch to close the crown.

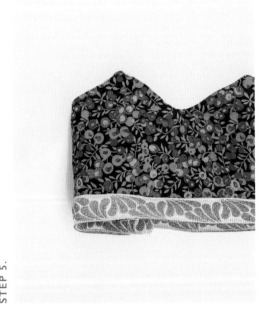

You can leave the crown as it is or, alternatively, sew a small pompom to each point.

MATERIALS & METHOD

FABRIC BIB

50 X 28 CM (20 X 11 IN) WHITE-AND-GOLD FABRIC
50 X 28 CM (20 X 11 IN) WHITE DOUBLE GAUZE
SEWING THEAD TO MATCH THE FABRIC
PAPER
PAPER AND FABRIC SCISSORS
PINS
SEWING MACHINE (OPTIONAL)
SEWING NEEDLE
IRON

As all parents know, mealtimes with babies and toddlers can be very messy affairs and you can never have too many bibs! This simple design doesn't take long to make – just be sure to choose easily washable fabrics, such as a poly-cotton blend or even a soft towelling.

STEP 1.

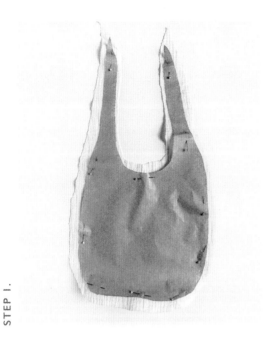

Photocopy the pattern on page 191, enlarged to 200%, and cut it out. Layer the two fabrics together, pin the pattern on top and cut out, cutting 1 cm (⅜ in) beyond the pattern. Remove the pattern.

STEP 2.

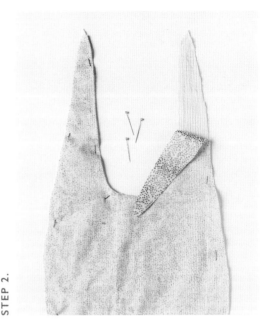

Place the two fabrics right sides together and sew all around by hand (using backstitch) or by machine, 1 cm (⅜ in) from the edge and leaving an 8-cm (3-in) opening at the bottom of the bib.

STEP 3.

Turn the bib right side out through the opening at the bottom.

STEP 4.

Fold under the edges of the opening and slipstitch the gap closed. Press the bib with the iron.

MATERIALS & METHOD

EMBROIDERED BIB

50 X 28 CM (20 X 11 IN) GREY LINEN
50 X 28 CM (20 X 11 IN) SOFT, EASY-TO-WASH FABRIC
TAPESTRY WOOL IN LIGHT BROWN, PALE YELLOW
AND PALE PINK
SEWING THREAD TO MATCH THE FABRIC
PAPER
TRACING PAPER
PENCIL
AIR- OR WATER-ERASABLE FABRIC MARKER
PEN (OPTIONAL)
PAPER AND FABRIC SCISSORS
EMBROIDERY HOOP
SHORT LENGTH OF THIN WIRE
PUNCH NEEDLE, 2.5 MM (1 IN) DIAMETER
PINS
SEWING MACHINE (OPTIONAL)
SEWING NEEDLE

This cheery little face is guaranteed to brighten up mealtimes.
Once you've mastered the technique, you could make several
bibs and embroider them with abstract designs of colourful
circles or stars instead.

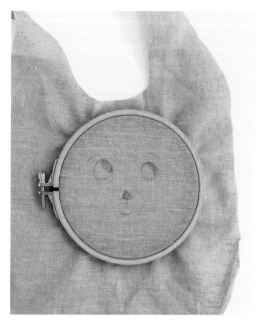

Photocopy the pattern on page 191, enlarged to 200%, and cut it out. Layer the linen and easy-to-wash fabrics together, pin the pattern on top and cut out the fabrics, 1 cm (⅜ in) beyond the edge of the pattern. Remove the pattern.

Photocopy one of the faces on pages 192–3, and place the grey linen over it so that the design is centred under the bib's collar. Trace the face onto the bib with a pencil or erasable fabric marker pen (see page 180). Place the grey linen in the hoop.

Choose your wool colours that you will embroider with the punch needle. You will need three different colours: one for embroidering the outline of the eyes, the pupils, the mouth, and the nose; one for the cheeks; and one to fill in the eyes.

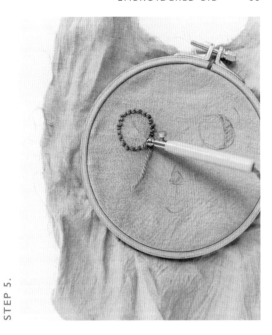

Thread the wool you have chosen for the eyes into the punch needle, using the piece of thin wire to help you (see page 24).

First, stitch the outline of the eyes using flat stitches (see pages 120–1).

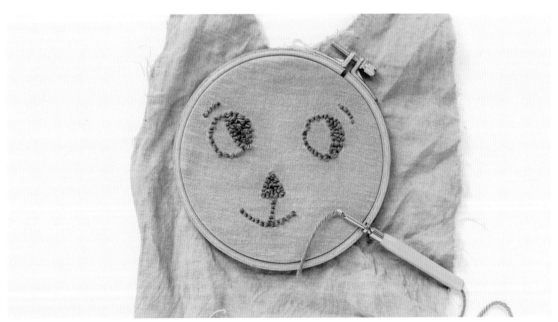

Fill in the pupils, then stitch the nose, mouth and eyebrows.

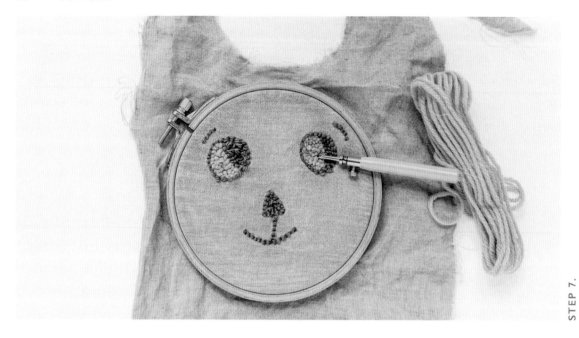

Using the pale yellow wool, finish filling in the eyes.

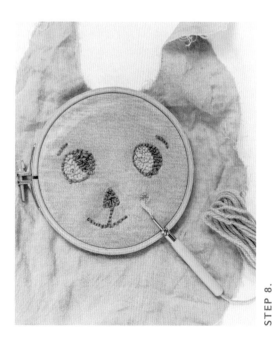

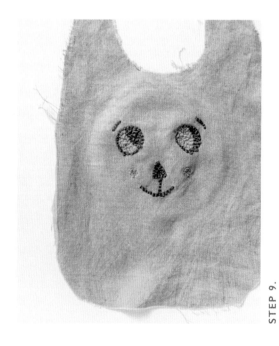

Embroider the little cheeks in pale pink.

Remove the embroidery hoop and press the linen on the reverse side. Assemble the bib following the instructions on page 81.

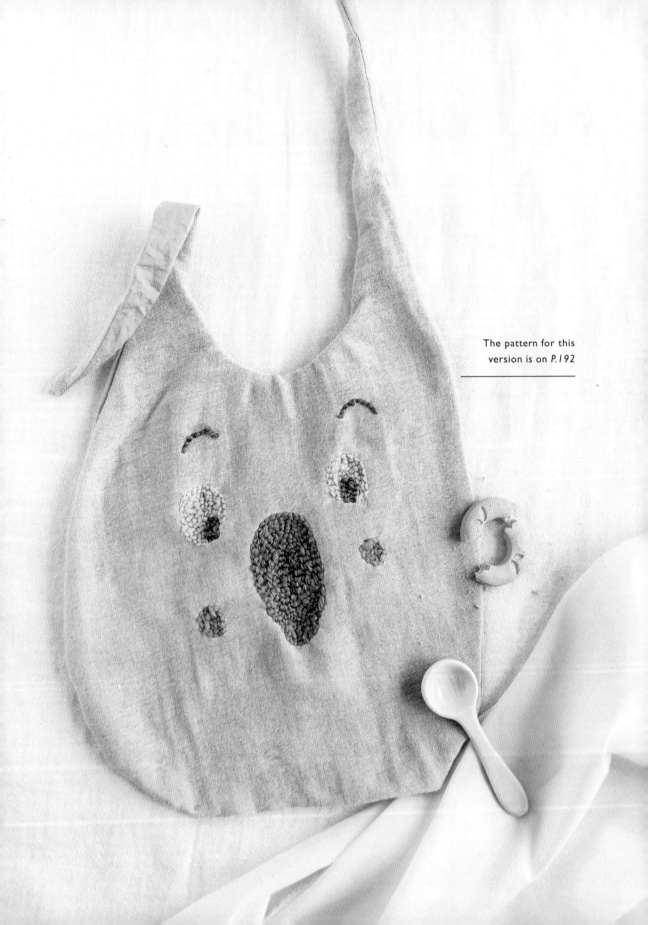

The pattern for this
version is on *P.192*

ON THE GO

MATERIALS & METHOD

NAPPY POUCH

30 X 21 CM (12 X 8¼ IN) AND 42 X 21 CM
(16½ X 8¼ IN) QUILTED FABRIC
SEWING THREAD TO MATCH THE FABRIC
70 CM (28 IN) GOLD BIAS BINDING
1 GOLD PRESS STUD
PAPER
PAPER AND FABRIC SCISSORS
PINS
SEWING MACHINE OR SEWING NEEDLE

When you're out and about with your baby, a nappy pouch is an essential. The ready-quilted fabric used here allows you to create a super stylish version. If you can't find a ready-quilted fabric you can, of course, quilt your own, as in the changing mat on page 100 – in which case, double the fabric amounts listed here and cut two pieces of lightweight wadding to the fabric sizes given opposite.

To be fully prepared, slip the portable baby changing mat on *P. 100* into your pouch.

Photocopy and cut out the patterns on page 194. Pin them to the quilted fabric and cut one front and one back piece. Place the fabric pieces right sides together. Sew together by hand (using backstitch) or by machine 0.5 cm (¼ in) from the edges.

Turn the pouch right side out and pin bias binding all around the flap, easing it around the curve. The bias binding hides the raw edges of the quilted fabric.

Next, pin bias binding along the opening. Stitch the binding in place about 3 mm (⅛ in) from the bottom edge of the binding. Do this either by hand using backstitch or by machine using a zigzag stitch.

Attach the press stud to the front and the flap. Press studs come in sew-on and no-sew versions; the no-sew ones often come in a kit with all the tools you'll need – follow the manufacturer's instructions.

Use the elastic
to slip the rug onto
your baby's high chair.

MATERIALS & METHOD

TEXTURED PLAY MAT

105 X 35 CM (42 X 14 IN) SWEATSHIRT FABRIC
22 FELT BALLS
SCRAPS OF IMITATION SHEEPSKIN, PINK LINEN AND
GOLD-AND-WHITE FABRIC
3 TASSELS
SEQUINS
50 X 35 CM (20 X 14 IN) WADDING
50 CM (20 IN) PALE PINK FLAT ELASTIC,
3 CM (1¼ IN) WIDE
STRONG WHITE SEWING THREAD
INVISIBLE SEWING THREAD
PAPER OR TRACING PAPER
PAPER AND FABRIC SCISSORS
IRON (OPTIONAL)
PINS
SEWING NEEDLE
SEWING MACHINE (OPTIONAL)

Round felt balls, soft silk tassels, fluffy imitation sheepskin –
there's a whole world of textures for tiny hands to explore
on this sensory play mat. Use the elastic loop on the back to
attach it to the tray of your baby's high chair.

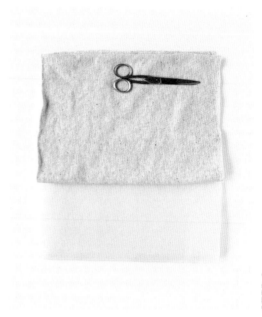

Tie a knot in one end of a length of strong white thread. Use the needle to thread the felt balls onto the white thread.

Cut the sweatshirt fabric in two widthways to create two 52.5 × 35-cm (21 × 14-in) pieces.

Prepare the decorative elements. Photocopy the templates on page 195 or trace them onto tracing paper using a pencil. Cut out the templates. Pin the cloud to the imitation sheepskin fabric, the mountain to the pink linen, and the two small triangles for the mountain tops to the gold fabric. Cut out the fabric pieces, following the outlines of the templates. You will also need tassels and sequins.

STEP 4.

STEP 5.

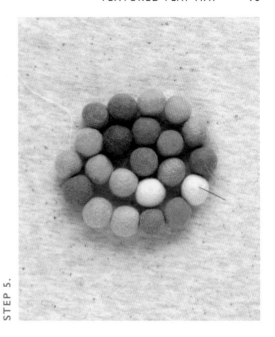

Sew the sequins on, one by one, at the bottom of the mountain, using invisible thread and making sure they are securely stitched.

Roll the string of felt balls into a spiral. Using invisible thread, sew them securely to one of the pieces of sweatshirt fabric, towards the right-hand side. Make sure they're really firmly attached.

STEP 6.

Sew the three tassels next to the felt balls. Place the cloud just above so that it hides the tops of the tassels. Stitch on the cloud using invisible thread.

Again using invisible thread, sew on the mountain to the left of the cloud, stitching on the white-and-gold mountain 'tops' as you go.

Place the two pieces of sweatshirt fabric right sides together, with the wadding on top. Use the white thread to sew around the edges by hand or machine 1 cm (⅜ in) from the edges. Leave an opening of about 10 cm (4 in) along the bottom edge.

Turn the mat the right side out through the opening. Flatten well, ironing around the shapes if necessary. Check once more that everything is firmly attached.

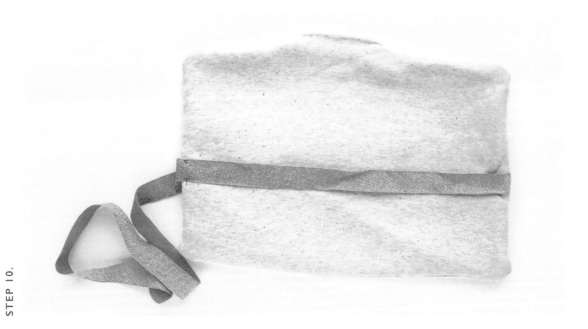

Fold one end of the elastic over by about 1 cm (⅜ in) and pin it to the front of the play mat, in the centre of one of the short sides of the mat. Turn the mat over and stretch the elastic over the back of the mat, keeping it flat and straight. This elastic ribbon will allow you to slip the mat over the tray of a high chair.

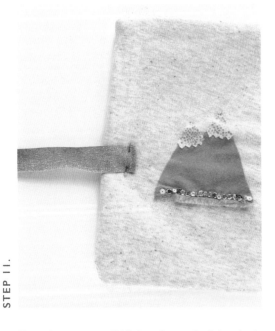

Turn the mat over. Fold the other end of the elastic over by about 1 cm (⅜ in) and pin it to the other short side of the front of the mat, as shown.

Sew the ends of the elastic to the fabric using white thread. Fold under the edges of the opening and slipstitch it closed, again using white thread.

MATERIALS & METHOD

PACIFIER CLIP

1 PACIFIER SUSPENDER CLIP ATTACHMENT (THESE CAN
BE BOUGHT IN PACKS ONLINE)
ASSORTED BEADS OF YOUR CHOICE
PACIFIER
60 CM (24 IN) OF STRONG THREAD
MASKING TAPE
SCISSORS

Pacifier clips are ideal when you're on the go as you can attach
them to a bib or pram to avoid the pacifier falling or getting
lost. You could also personalize the clip by using lettered beads
to spell out the baby's name.

Fold the thread in half, then pass the loop through the clip attachment. Pass the two ends of the thread through the loop and pull. Wrap masking tape around both ends of the thread to make it easier to thread the beads.

Thread the beads, alternating colours and shapes in any order you like. Different-sized beads work well, as well as beads in different colours and shapes for added texture.

With the remaining thread, make a large loop and then use a double knot to tie the thread very firmly up against the last bead. Pass this loop through the pacifier handle, then pass the clip and string of beads through the loop and pull.

For a neat finish, pass the end of the thread that's hanging off the loop back through the last bead and tie a single knot. Cut off any excess thread.

PORTABLE CHANGING MAT

60 X 60 CM (24 X 24 IN) FINE NEEDLECORD,
POWDER PINK
60 X 60 CM (24 X 24 IN) DOUBLE GAUZE, AQUA
60 X 60 CM (24 X 24 IN) WADDING
AQUA, PALE PINK AND GOLD SEWING THREAD
35 CM (14 IN) GLITTERY FLAT ELASTIC RIBBON,
3 CM (1¼ IN) WIDE
PINS
SEWING NEEDLE
SEWING MACHINE
IRON
RULER
PENCIL OR CHALK MARKER

This quilted changing mat rolls up into a neat, easily portable bundle that will fit into the nappy pouch on page 90. I've used a plain-coloured needlecord fabric to allow the quilting stitches to stand out well, but if you'd prefer a patterned fabric, you could find one with anything from big, bold flowers and geometric motifs to teddy bears and other cuddly creatures.

Place the two pieces of fabric right sides together, with the wadding on top.

Pin the three layers together, taking care not to crease them.

Sew all around by hand (using backstitch) or by machine, stitching 1 cm (⅜ in) from the edge and leaving a 10-cm (4-in) opening on one side.

STEP 4.

Turn right side out and use the iron to press thoroughly.

STEP 5.

Fold the edges of the opening inwards and slipstitch it closed.

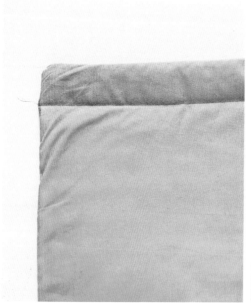

STEP 6.

STEP 7.

Thread the sewing machine, using aqua thread for the top thread and pale pink for the bobbin. Use a ruler and pencil to draw a straight line 4 cm (1½ in) from one edge. Sew along this line, backstitching at the start and finish.

Using the ruler and a chalk marker or pencil, draw parallel lines 4 cm (1½ in) apart lengthwise over the whole mat. Sew along these lines, again backstitching at the start and end of each line.

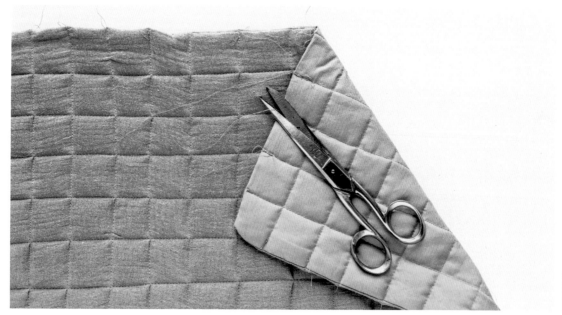

STEP 8.

Draw parallel lines 4 cm (1½ in) apart at right angles to the first set of lines and sew along them. When the grid pattern is complete, cut off the ends of any protruding threads.

STEP 9.

Overlap the ends of the elastic ribbon by 0.5 cm (¼ in) to form a circle and sew the ends together with the gold thread. Place the seam of the ribbon on one corner of the pink side of the mat and sew the elastic to the fabric.

STEP 10.

To fold the mat, lay it flat with the aqua side facing upwards and the elastic at the top. Fold the right and left corners into the centre. Starting at the bottom, roll the mat up and pull the elastic around it.

TO PLAY

MATERIALS & METHOD

TACTILE PICTURE FRAME

WOODEN PHOTO FRAME
HESSIAN FABRIC, 10 CM (4 IN) LONGER THAN THE
FRAME ON ALL SIDES
WOOL IN DIFFERENT COLOURS
CARDBOARD, SLIGHTLY SMALLER THAN THE FRAME'S
BACKING BOARD
PENCIL
EMBROIDERY HOOP
PUNCH NEEDLE
SCISSORS
IRON
MASKING TAPE

There are loads of sensory toys that you can buy, but it is more special to make your own unique one. You could even use up an old picture frame and some spare materials at the same time.

1. Open the frame and remove the glass and backing board. Place the frame on the fabric and, using the pencil, draw a line all round the inside of the frame – this will mark the visible area you will embroider.

2. Stretch the fabric over the embroidery hoop. Now you can create freestyle geometric shapes in different colours using the punch needle and wool (see pages 118–19 for how to thread the needle and pages 120–1 for the technique). If necessary, you can move the hoop around the fabric, but make sure you stay within the pencil line you have drawn.

3. When you have finished, remove the fabric from the hoop and press on the wrong side. Centre the piece of cardboard on the wrong side of the embroidery. Fold the edges of the fabric over the cardboard and secure them using masking tape. Place the embroidery-covered card face down in the frame and press the frame's backing board against the cardboard. Close the frame with the clips provided.

MATERIALS & METHOD

CUDDLY LLAMA

60 X 30 CM (24 X 12 IN) IMITATION SHEEPSKIN FABRIC
BLACK EMBROIDERY THREAD
WHITE SEWING THREAD
HOLLOWFIBRE STUFFING
SMALL AMOUNTS OF PINK AND WHITE WOOL ROVING
30 CM (12 IN) FRINGED RIBBON
PAPER
PAPER AND FABRIC SCISSORS
PINS
SEWING NEEDLE
SEWING MACHINE (OPTIONAL)
PENCIL
FELTING NEEDLE

With their long eyelashes and teddy-bear faces, llamas are undeniably cute! This adorable little toy is a great way to use up any imitation sheepskin left over from the waistcoat project on page 52.

STEP 1.

Photocopy the pattern on page 196, enlarged to 190%, and cut it out. Fold the imitation sheepskin fabric in half and pin the pattern onto the fabric. Cut the fabric to create two pieces, cutting 2 cm (¾ in) beyond the edge of the pattern.

STEP 2.

Sew a long straight stitch for each eye with a length of black embroidery thread. Firmly tie the two ends of the thread together on the wrong side.

STEP 3.

Pin the two parts of the llama right sides together. Using white thread, sew the two sides together by hand (using backstitch) or machine 2 cm (¾ in) from the edge. Leave an opening in the llama's belly for the stuffing. Turn the llama right side out.

STEP 4.

Stuff the llama, starting with the smaller parts such as the legs, ears and nose. Use a pencil to help you push the stuffing right into the corners. Fold the two sides of the opening inwards and slipstitch it closed.

Needle felt some white wool roving onto the head to create a small tuft between the llama's ears (see step 1 on page 21). As you pierce the wool repeatedly on the head, it will form a dense mass and become attached to the toy.

Needle felt some pink wool roving onto the cheeks.

Hand stitch the fringed ribbon around the middle of the llama's body using slipstitch.

STEP 2.

STEP 3.

MINI FINGER PUPPETS

THIN FELT IN SEVERAL COLOURS
GOLD EMBROIDERY THREAD
TRACING PAPER
PENCIL
PENCIL OR AIR- OR WATER-ERASABLE FABRIC
MARKER PEN (OPTIONAL)
FABRIC SCISSORS
EMBROIDERY NEEDLE
NON-TOXIC CRAFT GLUE (OPTIONAL)
BLACK PERMANENT FELT-TIP MARKER PEN

There are patterns on page 197 but, if you feel confident, you can draw some of your own shapes to create a whole cast of different characters. Making finger puppets is also a really fun activity to do with kids, once they are old enough.

1. Use a pencil to trace the shapes on page 197 onto tracing paper. Trace the shapes onto the felt with a pencil or erasable fabric marker pen (see page 180).

2. Cut out the same shape twice for each puppet, following the outlines of the templates. Place them together in pairs. Sew around the edges with a running stitch, using the embroidery needle and gold thread. Remember to leave the bottoms open. You can sew or glue on small pieces of felt in different colours to add extra detail, such as on the sun and the bird puppets.

3. To sew on small lines and details with the gold thread, slip a pen into each shape to prevent the needle piercing through both pieces of fabric at the same time. Sew these lines using running stitch. To create faces, draw on the eyes and mouth with a black permanent felt-tip pen.

You can find the pattern
for this version on *P. 198*.

MATERIALS & METHOD

SOFT CLOUD RATTLE

15 X 40 CM (6 X 16 IN) EMBROIDERY CANVAS,
7 THREADS PER CM
WOOL IN SEVERAL COLOURS
NARROW STRIPS OF VERY FINE FABRIC
VERY THICK COTTON THREAD
1 WOODEN RING, 6 CM (2½ IN) DIAMETER
VERY STRONG SEWING THREAD
HOLLOWFIBRE STUFFING
A FEW SMALL BELLS
TRACING PAPER
PENCIL
AIR- OR WATER-ERASABLE FABRIC MARKER
PEN (OPTIONAL)
EMBROIDERY HOOP
PUNCH NEEDLE
FABRIC SCISSORS
WOOL NEEDLE
PINS
SEWING NEEDLE

This cloud-shaped rattle, with its bright colours and little bells hidden inside, is sure to grab your baby's attention. Reaching to pick the rattle up will also help improve their hand–eye co-ordination.

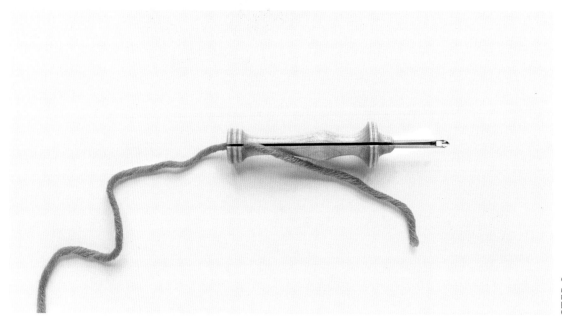

Transfer the outline of the cloud on page 198 onto the canvas (see page 180) in the upper part of the hoop. If you wish, you can mark out the individual sections of the cloud, too – or just work freehand. Stretch the canvas over the embroidery hoop.

Insert the end of a ball of mustard-coloured wool into the slot in the handle of the punch needle, at the opposite end from the needle.

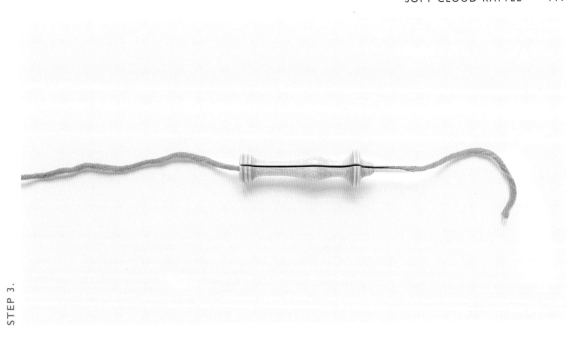

Slide the wool fully into the slot, so that it is perfectly positioned all along the handle of the punch needle. Pull on the wool gently so that it can slide easily.

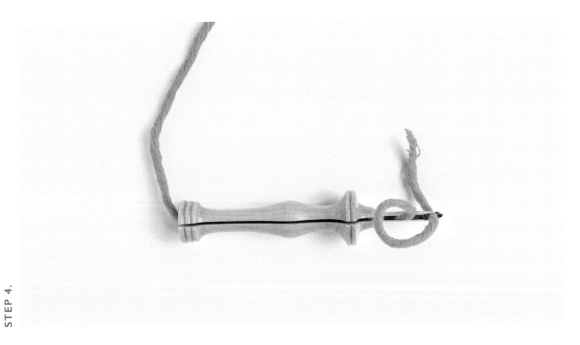

Thread the end of the wool through the eye of the needle. Then work with the open side of the needle facing the direction of the stitches you are making.

Insert the needle into the canvas, on the bottom left of the outline of the cloud. Pull gently on the punch needle so that it emerges just flush with the canvas, then insert it a little further on.

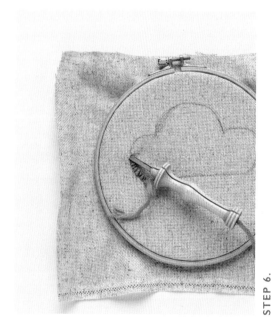

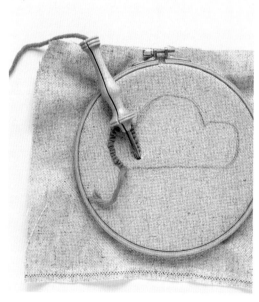

Repeat step 5 until you reach the end of the first part of the cloud, making all your stitches the same length.

Continue working around the outline of the mustard-yellow section until you reach the point where you started the embroidery. Now fill in this area, embroidering in a circular fashion from the outside inwards.

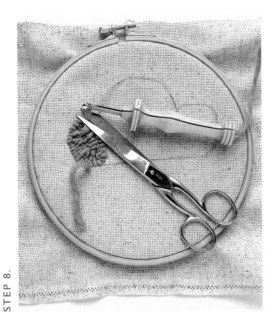

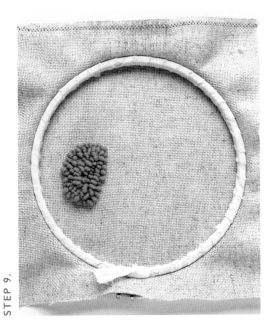

When the area is completely filled, pull gently on the punch needle and cut the thread flush with the canvas.

Small loops will have formed on the other side of the embroidery.

Using the pink wool, outline another area, next to the mustard-coloured one, and fill it in as before.

Repeat with the sky-blue wool, just below the pink area. You can also embroider a few areas using fine strips of fabric to add a different texture – just thread the fabric through the punch needle in exactly the same way as the wool.

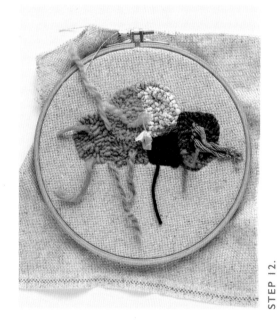

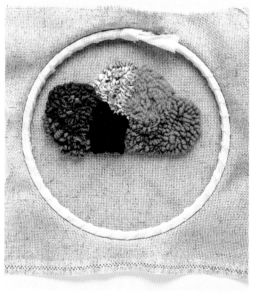

Finish filling in the cloud using the other colours. Tie together any protruding threads to finish off your work.

Turn the hoop over and remove the fabric from the hoop.

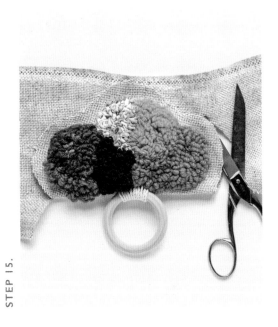

Thread a wool needle with thick cotton thread. With the loops facing you, insert the needle into the canvas, under the embroidery. Push the point of the needle back through the wooden ring.

When you have sewn about 10 stitches round the ring, fasten off the thread at the back. Fold the canvas in two, then cut out the cloud shape, cutting through both layers about 2 cm (¾ in) beyond the embroidery.

Fold the raw edges of both layers of fabric in and pin in place. Use the sewing needle and strong sewing thread to slipstitch the back and front layers of canvas together, leaving a small opening. Fill the rattle with hollowfibre stuffing and slip the bells inside. Slipstitch the opening closed.

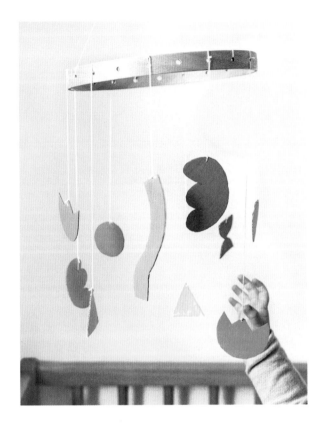

MATERIALS & METHOD

GEOMETRIC MOBILE

THICK WHITE CARDBOARD
PAINTS IN DIFFERENT COLOURS
PAINTBRUSH
STRONG COTTON THREAD
WOODEN CIRCULAR WEAVING FRAME
I WOODEN BEAD
PAPER
PENCIL
SCISSORS
SEWING NEEDLE

Babies begin to see colours between about four and six months of age, so this is the perfect time to create a mobile to hang above your baby's cot. This easy-to-make design features eye-catching bright colours and bold shapes.

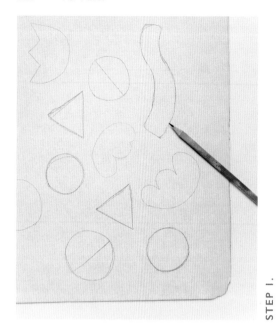

STEP 1.

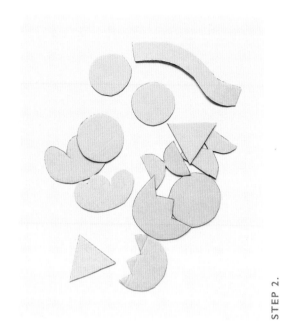

STEP 2.

Photocopy the shapes on page 199, enlarged to 200%, and cut them out. Use a pencil to draw around the shapes onto thick white cardboard.

Cut out the shapes from the cardboard using a pair of scissors.

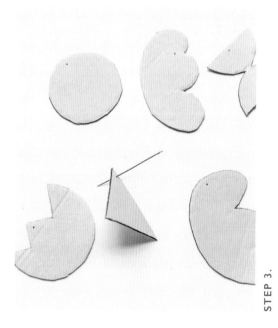

STEP 3.

STEP 4.

With a needle, make a hole in the top of each shape.

Paint the front and back of each shape.

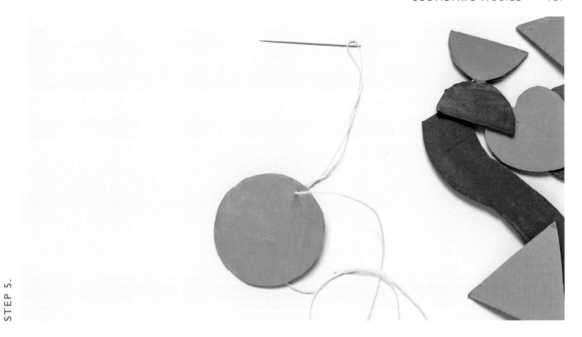

Thread a length of cotton thread with a knot at the end through each shape. Use different lengths of thread.

Slide each shape to the end of its length of thread and push it against the knot. Pass the other end of the thread through a hole in the wooden circle and tie a knot to attach it. Attach a shape to every other hole around the circle.

Use the remaining holes to add four lengths of cotton thread of the same length, spaced at regular intervals. Tie these threads together, pass them through a wooden bead and tie the ends together again on the other side of the bead.

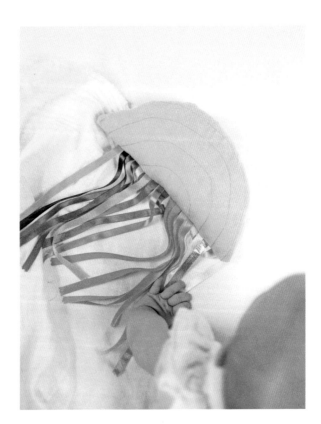

MATERIALS & METHOD

RAINBOW SOFT TOY

26 X 32 CM (10½ X 12½ IN) POWDER-PINK GAUZE
ASSORTED RIBBONS, 22 CM (9 IN) LONG IN
DIFFERENT COLOURS
GOLD SEWING THREAD
SEWING THREAD TO MATCH THE FABRIC
HOLLOWFIBRE STUFFING
PAPER
PAPER AND FABRIC SCISSORS
PINS
ADHESIVE TAPE
SEWING MACHINE
SEWING NEEDLE

Every colour in the rainbow spills out of this soft toy. Babies will love twisting the ribbons around their little fingers – and the squishy rainbow shape itself can even double up as a miniature pillow when they're tired of playing.

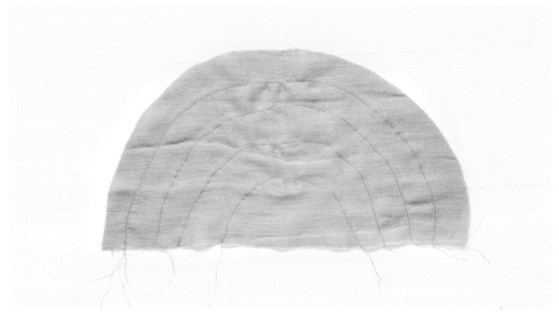

Photocopy and cut out the template on page 200 and pin it to the fabric. Cut two pieces from the fabric, following the outline of the template. On one of the pieces, machine stitch some arcs, 3 cm (1¼ in) apart, in gold thread. Don't stitch too close to the top of the semicircle, otherwise your stitches will disappear in the seam allowance when you stitch the pieces together in step 4.

Line up the ribbons in order of colour and stick a piece of adhesive tape across one end. Turn the ribbons over and stick another piece of tape on top. Stitch a line through the adhesive tape to join the ribbons. Remove the tape.

Place the two semicircles right sides together and slip the ribbons between the two pieces of fabric. Line up the tops of the ribbons with the straight edges of the semicircles. Sew across, 1 cm (⅜ in) from the straight edges, to fix the ribbons in place.

Put the ribbons inside the semicircles and sew around the curve 1 cm (⅜ in) from the edge. Leave an opening of about 10 cm (4 in) in one side. Take care not to catch the ribbons in the seam.

Turn the toy right side out through the opening so that the ribbons hang down.

Fill the toy with the hollowfibre stuffing. Fold the edges of the opening inwards and slipstitch it closed by hand.

MATERIALS & METHOD

LITTLE TEDDY BEAR

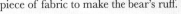

55 X 20 CM (22 X 8 IN) BOILED WOOL FABRIC
BLACK EMBROIDERY THREAD
SEWING THREAD TO MATCH
THE FABRIC
HOLLOWFIBRE STUFFING
15 X 8 CM (6 X 3 IN) GOLDEN TULLE
GOLD EMBROIDERY THREAD
1 SMALL HAT (SEE PAGE 134)
PAPER
PAPER AND FABRIC SCISSORS
PINS
SEWING NEEDLE
PENCIL

Once you've got the hang of this project, you could sew
several bears in different colours to make enough for a teddy
bears' picnic! If you don't have any golden tulle, use a spare
piece of fabric to make the bear's ruff.

STEP 1.

STEP 2.

Photocopy the pattern on page 201, enlarged to 210%, and cut it out. Fold the fabric in two lengthways. Pin the pattern onto it and cut out the fabric, following the outline of the pattern.

Refer to the photo to embroider eyes and a nose in black thread on one piece. Knot the thread on the reverse. Place the two pieces right sides together and sew together about 5 mm (¼ in) from the edges using sewing thread. Leave an opening for the stuffing.

STEP 3.

STEP 4.

Turn the bear right side out. Fill the bear with hollowfibre stuffing. Use a pencil to help you push the stuffing into the ends of the paws. Slipstitch the opening closed.

Using gold thread, sew a line of running stitches along one long edge of the golden tulle and gather the fabric to form a ruff. Place the ruff around the bear's neck and tie the thread at the back. Sew the hat onto the bear's head.

MATERIALS & METHOD

CUSTOMIZE YOUR TEDDY BEAR

PATTERNED PAPER
SMALL POMPOMS
RIBBON WITH POMPOMS
SCISSORS
NON-TOXIC CRAFT GLUE
SEWING NEEDLE
SEWING THREAD

You can also add accessories to your teddy bear. These instructions show you how to make a hat, but you can get creative and add a scarf, clothes and more…

1. To make a little hat, cut a semicircle from some pretty paper. Apply a line of glue along the right-hand edge, on the wrong side of the paper, then roll up the semicircle to make a cone. Press the glued edge to the opposite edge.

2. Glue a small pompom to the point of the hat, and some ribbon with pompoms all around the hat's inner edge. You can then sew the pompoms onto the soft toy's head to attach the hat.

MATERIALS & METHOD

LUCKY CHARMS

2 PIECES OF COTTON FABRIC, 15 X 15 CM (6 X 6 IN)
EMBROIDERY THREAD IN SEVERAL DIFFERENT COLOURS
SEWING THREAD TO MATCH THE FABRIC
HOLLOWFIBRE STUFFING
TRACING PAPER
PENCIL
AIR- OR WATER-ERASABLE FABRIC
MARKER PEN (OPTIONAL)
EMBROIDERY HOOP
MAGIC EMBROIDERY PEN
SMALL LENGTH OF THIN WIRE
FABRIC SCISSORS
SEWING NEEDLE

These lucky charms are the perfect size for little hands to grasp and they're really quick and easy to make. You could also make them into a mobile to hang above your baby's cot or a garland to string across a pram.

Transfer one of the motifs on page 180 onto the piece of cotton fabric (also refer to the instructions on page 180 for transferring motifs). Stretch the fabric over the embroidery hoop.

Thread the magic embroidery pen using the thin wire (see page 24). On the wrong side of the fabric, embroider the cheeks of the lucky charm using embroidery thread (see pages 120–1).

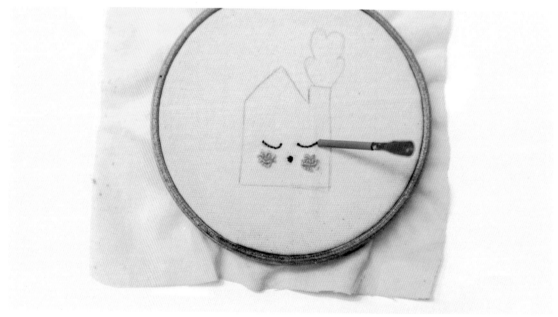

On the right side of the fabric, embroider the eyelids and a nose.

STEP 4.

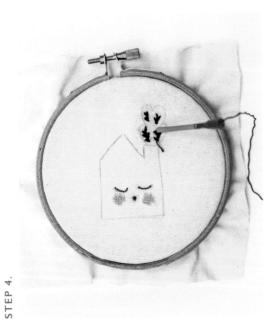

On the right side of the hoop, embroider small details such as a door, some smoke or a border. Refer to the photos on pages 136–7 and the designs on page 180.

STEP 5.

Remove the embroidery from the hoop and cut the fabric all around, leaving a 5 mm (¼ in) margin around the embroidery.

STEP 6.

Cut another piece of fabric to the same size. Place the two pieces right sides together and sew all around using the sewing thread, 5 mm (¼ in) from the edges. Leave an opening for the stuffing.

STEP 7.

Turn the charm right side out and fill it with hollowfibre stuffing. Use a pencil to help you push the stuffing into smaller areas such as the chimney. Slipstitch the opening closed. Repeat all the steps with the other shapes.

MATERIALS & METHOD

MACRAMÉ TOY

30 PIECES OF CORD, 45 CM (18 IN) LONG
WOODEN RING, 6 CM (2½ IN) DIAMETER
FINE, STRONG COTTON THREAD
SCISSORS
WOOL NEEDLE

This is another touch-and-feel toy that your baby will love to pick up and play with: the solid cords and knots around the central ring contrast with the soft, fringed cord ends. In macramé the threads are knotted, rather than stitched or woven, to create decorative patterns. It might look complicated, but once you have mastered a few basic knots you'll find that it is actually a very easy technique.

Make a loop in a piece of cord, leaving one end longer than the other. Slide the loop under the ring, thread the two ends through the loop and pull. Tie a second piece of cord in the same way, but reversing the lengths of its ends, so that the shorter lengths are on the inside.

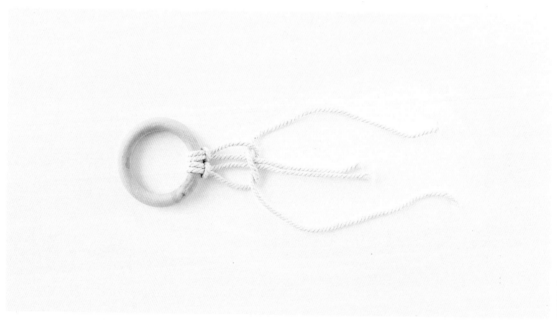

To tie the first knot, pass the left-hand end over the two middle ends, then under the right-hand end. Pass the right-hand end under the two middle ends, then thread it through the loop that has been formed on the left. Pull on these two ends to tighten the knot.

Tie a total of eight knots as described in step 2, then tie a final normal knot on the right and on the left.

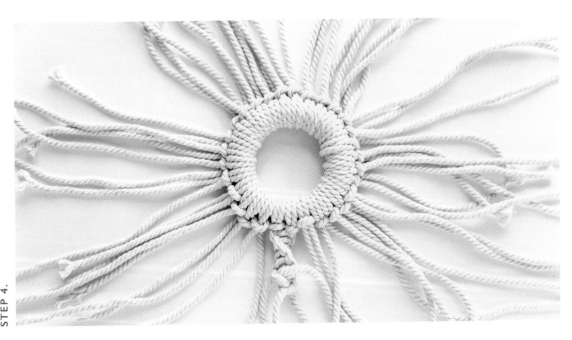

Tie the other 28 pieces of cord around the ring in the same way. Tie eight knots with each piece, as described in step 2, and fix them with a final knot.

Cut the cords 1 cm (⅜ in) from the knots.

Pull the ends of the cords to fray them 1 cm (⅜ in) at the ends of the cords.

Use a wool needle to thread some fine cotton thread through the knots.

Pull on the cotton thread to tighten the knots, then tie the ends of the cotton thread together in a really firm knot.

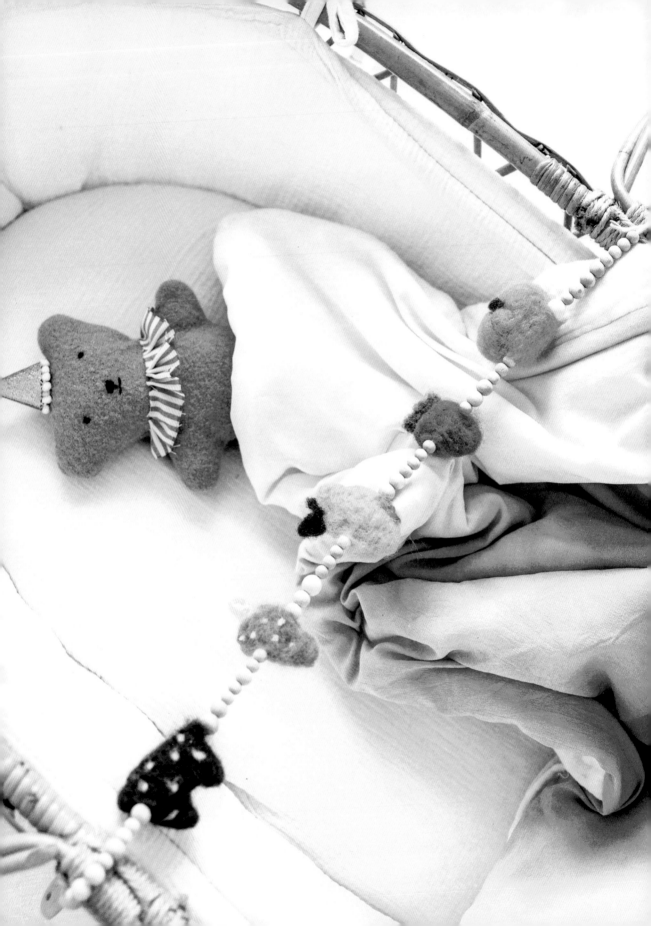

MATERIALS & METHOD

CRIB GARLAND

THICK COTTON THREAD OR THIN ELASTIC
2 PACIFIER CLIP ATTACHMENTS
ROUND WOODEN BEADS IN DIFFERENT SIZES
WOOL TOPS OR ROVING IN DIFFERENT COLOURS
FOAM BLOCK
FELTING NEEDLE

Colourful needle-felted shapes make a really eye-catching garland, and once you've mastered the technique you can make each one in a matter of minutes. You could also hang this toy from a Moses basket or the hood of a pushchair.

1. Fold a length of cotton thread in half and thread the loop through the fastening of a pacifier clip attachment. Thread the two thread ends through the loop, and pull to firmly attach the thread to the clip. Alternatively, use thin elastic and stitch the end around the pacifier clip. Thread about 15 wooden beads of varying sizes onto the double thread or elastic.

2. Refer to the motifs on page 197 to help you make your needle-felted shapes. Place some purple wool roving on the foam block and work it repeatedly with the felting needle to form the mountain shape (see step 1 on page 21). Lay the double threads onto the wool shape and use the felting needle to push it into the wool and attach the shape to the thread. Continue felting, adding a little more purple roving to mask the threads. The more you work it, the firmer and better defined the shape will be.

3. Add small dots of white wool roving to the mountain shape. Pierce the white wool repeatedly with the felting needle to attach it to the purple roving. Thread some more beads onto the thread. Continue felting shapes and threading beads in the same way. Once you come to the end of the thread, attach the ends of the thread firmly to a second pacifier clip attachment, tying several knots.

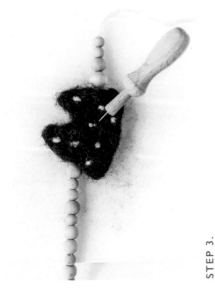

MATERIALS & METHOD

WOOLLY RATTLES

3 TRANSPARENT PLASTIC BALLS – 2 SMALL, 1 LARGE
SMALL BELLS
WOOL IN DIFFERENT COLOURS AND THICKNESSES
GOLD THREAD
ADHESIVE TAPE
SCISSORS

Filled with jingling bells, wrapped in tactile yarns in an array of pastel hues, these easy-to-construct little toys will appeal to babies' sense of sight, touch and hearing – a simple and fun way to help their development.

Place several bells inside a transparent ball and close it firmly.

Tape the ball all around its opening to seal it.

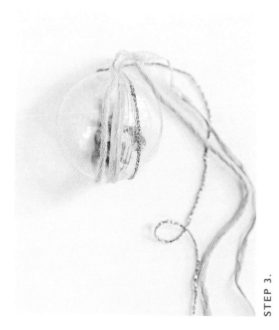

Tape three lengths of wool around the ball. Choose colours that blend harmoniously. You could also add a length of gold thread for contrast.

Completely cover the ball with the wool, taping it as you go along on all sides to keep the threads firmly in place.

Continue covering the ball with wool (now without taping it), crossing the lengths in a random way – diagonally, horizontally, and so on.

When the ball is completely covered with wool, cut the wool and tie it firmly to several strands of wool to secure it in place. Repeat all the steps with the other two transparent balls. Check that the threads are secure before giving the rattles to a child.

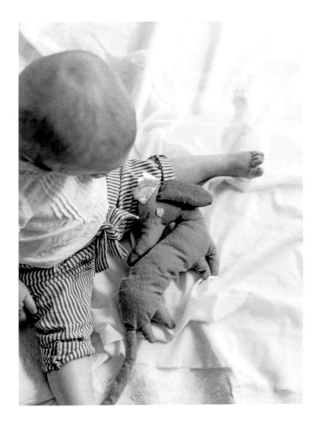

MATERIALS & METHOD

SLEEPY SAUSAGE DOG

2 PIECES OF 45 X 30 CM (18 X 12 IN) BROWN FABRIC
20 X 5 CM (8 X 2 IN) FINE DARK BLUE FABRIC
4 X 4 CM (1 ½ X 1 ½ IN) PINK LINEN
10 X 10 CM (4 X 4 IN) GOLD FABRIC
20 X 10 CM (8 X 4 IN) WADDING
THICK BLACK EMBROIDERY THREAD
SEWING THREAD TO MATCH THE FABRIC
HOLLOWFIBRE STUFFING
PAPER
PAPER AND FABRIC SCISSORS
PENCIL
PINS
SEWING NEEDLE
SEWING MACHINE (OPTIONAL)

Gently snoozing, with their eyes tightly shut, this cute sausage dog makes a cuddly companion for your little one. This toy has a gold crown, but you can invent your own accessories – perhaps you could tie a miniature version of a bow from page 62 around its neck.

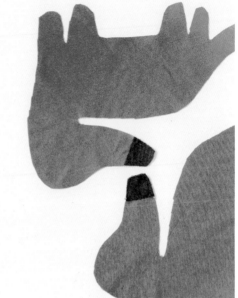

Photocopy the pattern on page 202, enlarged to 170%, and cut it out. Place two pieces of brown fabric together, pin the pattern on top, and cut the fabric 2 cm (¾ in) beyond the edge of the pattern.

Again using the pattern as a guide and cutting 2 cm (¾ in) beyond the edge, cut two nose-shaped pieces from the blue fabric. Place these at the end of the nose on each piece and sew around their edges.

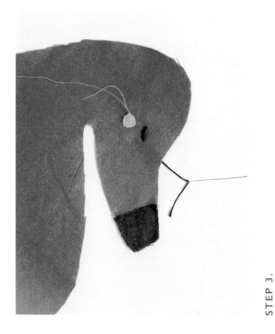

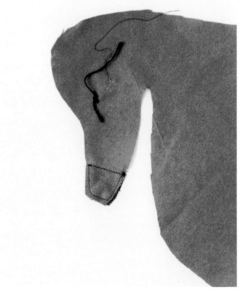

Cut two circles from the pink linen and sew them onto the head to make cheeks. Use a length of black embroidery thread to sew a long straight stitch for each eye.

On the wrong side of each piece, firmly tie together the two ends of the black thread. Place the two parts of the dog right sides together and sew all around by hand (using backstitch) or machine 2 cm (¾ in) from the edge, leaving an opening for the stuffing.

STEP 5.

STEP 6.

Turn the dog right side out.

Stuff the soft toy, starting with the tail, the paws and other extremities. Use the end of a pencil to push the stuffing in firmly, then fill the body. Slipstitch the opening shut.

STEP 7.

Cut four ear shapes from the blue fabric and two from the wadding. Then cut two crown shapes from the gold fabric and one from wadding. Place the pieces of fabric together in pairs, right sides together, with the wadding on top. Sew around the shapes by hand (using backstitch) or machine 2 cm (¾ in) from the edges. Leave the tops of the ears and the right-hand side of the crown open. Turn the ears and crown right side out, and slipstitch the openings shut. Pin the ears and crown onto the head and then sew them in place.

FOR BEDTIME

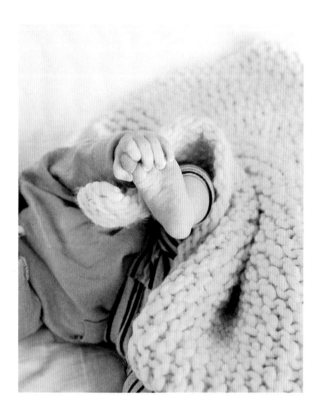

MATERIALS & METHOD

SNUGGLY KNITTED BLANKET

6 X 100 G (3.5 OZ) BALLS OF SUPER CHUNKY
ÉCRU YARN
1 PAIR OF 10-MM (US 15) KNITTING NEEDLES
WOOL NEEDLE

If you're new to knitting or short of time, this cosy blanket is the perfect project for you – chunky yarn and large knitting needles make it a cinch to knit.

If you're new to knitting then take this project slowly to begin with. Start by casting on the stitches.

Cast on 70 stitches in all.

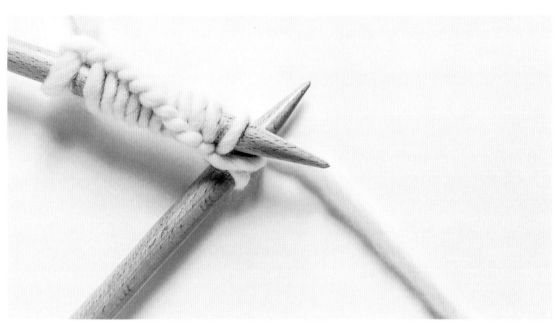

Knit one, then purl one.

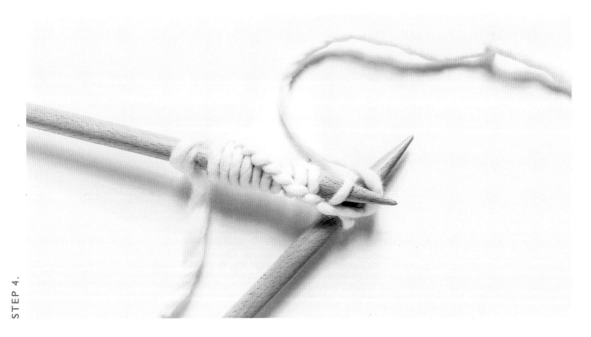

STEP 4.

Continue to knit one, purl one to the end of the row.

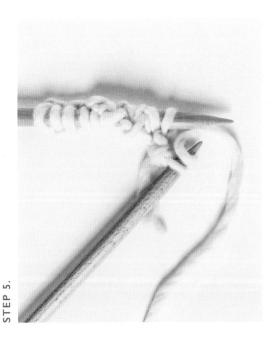

STEP 5.

STEP 6.

On the next row, purl one, knit one to the end of the row. Repeat these two rows until the work measures about 120 cm (48 in), then cast off as follows.

Knit two stitches, slide the left needle into the first knitted stitch, and pass it over the second. Continue along the whole row. When just one stitch remains, cut the wool, pass it through the stitch, and pull. Weave in the yarn ends with the wool needle.

MATERIALS & METHOD

COSY SLEEP SACK

TWO 90 X 55-CM (36 X 22-IN) PIECES OF AQUA
DOUBLE GAUZE
TWO 90 X 55-CM (36 X 22-IN) PIECES OF DOUBLE
GAUZE, DARK GREEN WITH GOLD POLKA DOTS
TWO 90 X 55-CM (36 X 22-IN) PIECES OF WADDING
SEWING THREAD TO MATCH THE FABRIC
120-CM (48-IN) ZIP, AQUA
2 GOLD PRESS STUDS
PAPER
PENCIL
PAPER AND FABRIC SCISSORS
PINS
SEWING MACHINE
ZIPPER FOOT FOR SEWING MACHINE (OPTIONAL)
SEWING NEEDLE

Sweet dreams are guaranteed with this cosy quilted sleeping bag. You can personalize it by embroidering your baby's name on a separate piece of fabric, as in the cushion on page 16, and sewing it on.

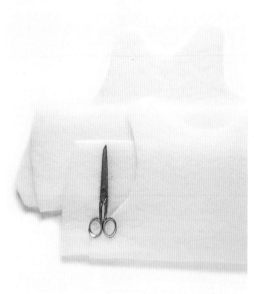

STEP 1.

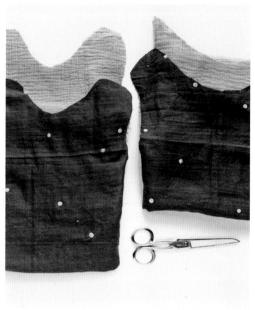

STEP 2.

Photocopy the pattern on page 203, enlarged to 200%, and cut out the pieces. Pin the patterns on the wadding and, with a pencil, extend the length by 45 cm (18 in) or by the baby's height. Cut the wadding 1 cm (⅜ in) beyond the edges of the pattern.

Using the same patterns, cut the back and front from the aqua double gauze, again cutting 1 cm (⅜ in) beyond the pattern. Do the same with the dark green double gauze.

STEP 3.

Start by making the back of the sleep sack. Place the aqua lining back piece and the dark green back piece right sides together, with the corresponding wadding piece on top. Pin all three layers together.

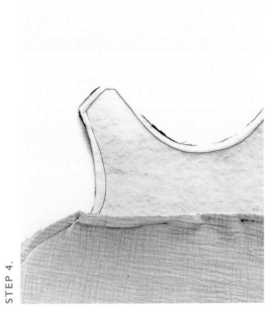

STEP 4.

Sew all around, taking a 1-cm (⅜-in) seam allowance and leaving a 10–15-cm (4–6-in) opening in the bottom edge.

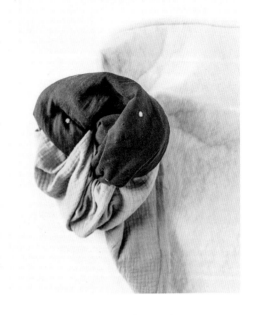

STEP 5.

Turn right side out through the opening.

STEP 6.

Fold the edges of the opening inwards and slipstitch it closed.

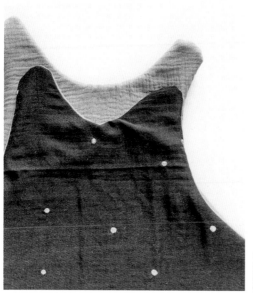

Make the front of the sleep sack in the same way: sew together the three layers, turn right side out and then sew the opening shut.

Pin one side edge of the back and front of the sleep sack right sides together.

Stitch along this side edge of the sleep sack, following the line of the pins and stitching 2–3 mm (⅛ in) from the edge.

Open the zip and pin each side of the zip tape to the unstitched side of the sleep sack, as shown above. Sew it on. Stitch as close to the zip teeth as possible, without stitching over them; it helps if your machine has a zipper foot for this, but if it doesn't just take your time.

Attach two press studs to the shoulder straps, taking care to attach the back ones the right way – the front shoulder straps fold over the back straps to close. Press studs come in sew-on and no-sew versions; the no-sew ones often come in a kit with all the tools you'll need – follow the manufacturer's instructions.

Press the studs together to close the sleep sack.

MATERIALS & METHOD

CUDDLY LION BLANKET

30 X 15 CM (12 X 6 IN) CREAM COTTON FABRIC
28 X 35 CM (11 X 14 IN) CREAM DOUBLE GAUZE
28 X 35 CM (11 X 14 IN) PATTERNED FABRIC
EMBROIDERY THREAD IN MUSTARD, PALE PINK,
BROWN, BLACK AND GREY
YARN IN MUSTARD
SEWING THREAD TO MATCH THE FABRIC
EMBROIDERY HOOP
TRACING PAPER
PENCIL
AIR- OR WATER-ERASABLE MARKER PEN (OPTIONAL)
MAGIC EMBROIDERY PEN
FABRIC SCISSORS
SEWING NEEDLE
SEWING MACHINE (OPTIONAL)
ADHESIVE TAPE
HOLLOWFIBRE STUFFING

This 'king of the jungle' looks pretty friendly! His smiley face and shaggy mane give him bags of character and make him an adorable bedtime toy for your child.

STEP 1.

Using a pencil or erasable marker pen, transfer the design on page 204 onto the fabric (see page 180). Stretch the cotton fabric over the embroidery hoop. Embroider the design using the magic embroidery pen. Sew on the right side of the fabric for the eyes, eyebrows, mouth and the bridge of the nose (see pages 120–1). Embroider on the wrong side of the fabric for the cheeks and nose. Remove the fabric from the hoop.

STEP 2.

STEP 3.

Cut about 70 pieces of mustard-coloured yarn, 10 cm (4 in) long.

Cut the fabric all around the face, leaving at least 4 cm (1½ in) around the embroidery. Cut a piece of cotton the same size for the back as well.

STEP 4.

STEP 5.

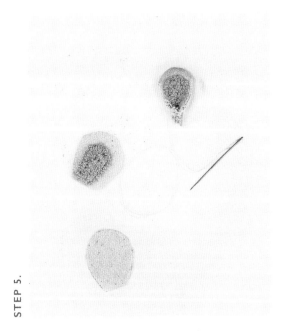

Transfer the fronts and backs of the two ears onto another piece of cotton fabric using your pencil or erasable fabric marker pen. Stretch the fabric over the hoop. Embroider the centre of the ears in pale pink, working on the wrong side of the fabric.

Cut out the ears, 5 mm (¼ in) beyond the outlines. Place them right sides together in pairs, then stitch all around by hand (using backstitch) 5 mm (¼ in) from the edge of the fabric. Leave the bottom edges open. Turn the ears right side out. Fold the bottom edges in half and secure with a stitch.

STEP 6.

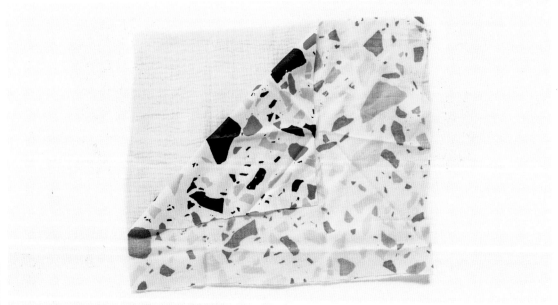

Place the double gauze and patterned fabric right sides together and stitch all around by hand (using backstitch) or machine. Stitch 1 cm (⅜ in) from the edges and leave a 10-cm (4-in) opening in the middle of one side. Turn right side out.

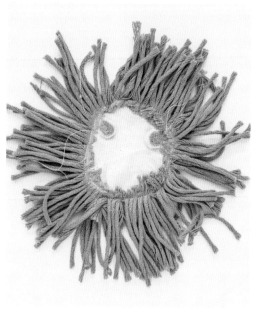

Turn the edges of the opening in and slipstitch it closed.

Position the ears, with the embroidered sides facing you, on either side of the top of the back of the head. Place the pieces of yarn all around the back of the head. Tape the wool and ears in place, then sew them onto the head.

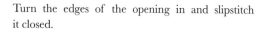

Fold all the pieces of yarn in towards the middle of the head and sew all around the edge once more, so that the wool is kept inside.

Sew the fabric rectangle onto the bottom of the back of the head, over the yarn.

Place the front of the face on the back of the face, with the back of the embroidery facing you. Sew all around by hand or machine 5 mm (¼ in) from the edge. Leave an opening at the neck. Turn the head right side out.

Fill the lion's head with hollowfibre stuffing. Turn under the edges of the opening in the neck and slipstitch it closed.

Trim the lion's mane to make it an even length all the way around.

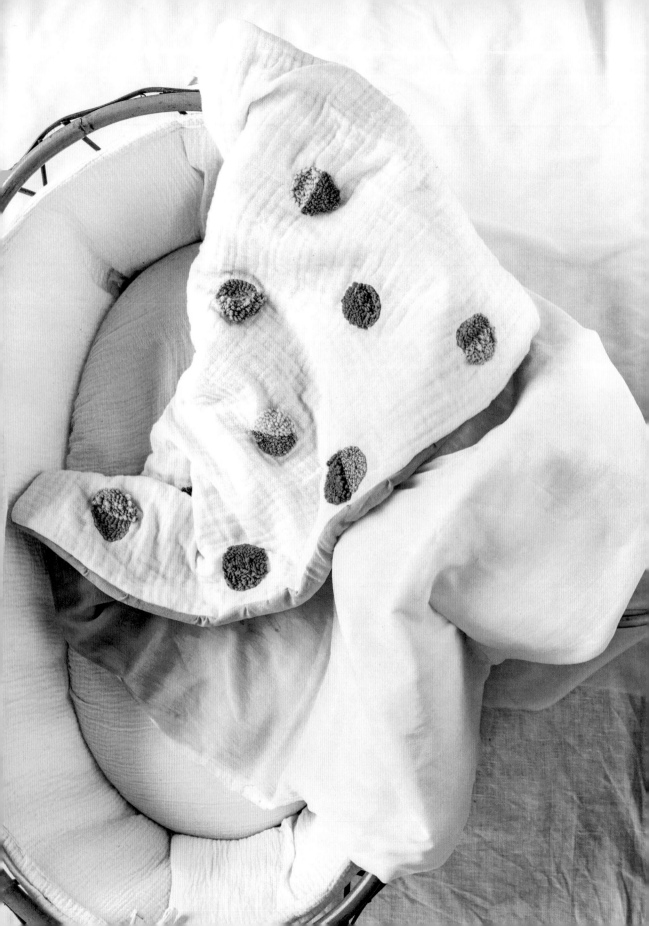

MATERIALS & METHOD

DYED QUILT

105 X 85 CM (41 X 33½ IN) WHITE LINEN OR MUSLIN
AVOCADO PEEL AND STONES
105 X 85 CM (41 X 33½ IN) DOUBLE GAUZE
TAPESTRY WOOL IN POWDER PINK, GOLD, LIGHT
GREEN, TERRACOTTA, GREY, MUSTARD AND DARK PINK
105 X 85 CM (41 X 33½ IN) THIN WADDING
SEWING THREAD TO MATCH THE FABRIC
CONTAINER FOR WATER
SAUCEPAN
SIEVE OR COLANDER
IRON
PUNCH NEEDLE, 2.5 MM DIAMETER
SHORT LENGTH OF THIN WIRE
EMBROIDERY HOOP
PINS
SEWING NEEDLE OR SEWING MACHINE

Dip-dyeing, where different parts of the fabric are given different intensities of colour, is a simple but very effective technique. This project eschews harsh chemical dyes in favour of a natural dye made from avocado stones and peel that would otherwise be thrown away.

Immerse the linen or muslin in a container filled with water to soak it completely, then drain away the excess water.

Scrape and wash the avocado peelings and stones to remove all of the green flesh. Place them in a large saucepan and cover with water. Bring to the boil and simmer for half an hour.

Use a sieve or colander to strain the water that has been coloured with the avocado peel and stones, pour it back into the saucepan, and put it back on the stove. Immerse three quarters of the linen or muslin in the saucepan for 10 minutes.

Remove part of the fabric from the saucepan, leaving only a third of it in the water. Leave it in the saucepan for about 10 minutes, still on the heat. As the water evaporates from the saucepan, the colour will become stronger.

Remove the fabric from the saucepan and rinse it in clean, cold water.

Remove the fabric from the cold water and wring it out. Rinse it under a tap and leave it to dry, preferably flat and outdoors. Press with an iron to get rid of any creases.

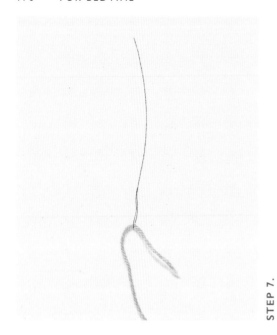

To make it easier to thread the punch needle, pass the end of the thread through a loop of fine wire.

Pass the wire through the punch needle, from the bottom to the top, and pull until the embroidery thread comes through.

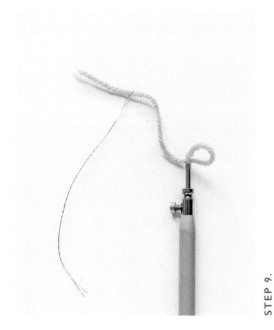

Pass the wire through the eye of the needle and pull on it to pull the embroidery thread through as well.

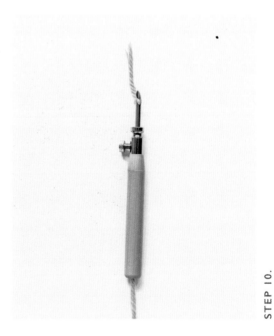

Remove the wire and pull on the thread slightly so that it is taut.

Stretch a small section of the fabric over an embroidery hoop. Embroider a pink semicircle with the punch needle on the right side of the fabric (see pages 120–1).

Embroider the adjoining semicircle with light green thread on the wrong side of the hoop. Repeat steps 11 and 12 randomly across the blanket, using different-coloured tapestry wool.

Place the two fabric rectangles right sides together, with the wadding on top. Pin together and sew all around by hand or machine 1 cm (⅜ in) from the edges. Leaving a 15–20-cm (6–8-in) opening in the middle of one side. Turn right side out and slipstitch the opening closed.

PATTERNS & TEMPLATES

Here are the patterns and templates you will need to make the projects in this book. Refer to the page number next to the pattern or template to find the relevant project instructions.

For the sewing patterns, you need only photocopy them and cut them out (the patterns specify whether you need to enlarge them and by how much). For the patterns that are their actual size, if you do not have a photocopier, trace them onto tracing paper. Pin the tracing paper to a piece of kraft paper or pattern paper, and then cut the pattern out.

To transfer a motif or embroidery pattern onto fabric, enlarge it to the required size if necessary, then trace it onto tracing paper. If your fabric is light coloured, tape the tracing over a light source (a light box, if you have one, or a window), then tape the fabric on top. Go over the tracing lines with an erasable fabric marker pen or a pencil.

If your fabric is dark coloured, enlarge the design if necessary and trace the motif onto tracing paper. Cut a piece of dressmaker's carbon paper about the same size as your design. This comes in several colours, so choose one that contrasts with your fabric. Place the coloured side of the carbon paper down on the fabric, then pin the tracing paper with the design on top. On a hard surface, go over the lines with a biro top, pressing firmly but not so hard that you tear the tracing paper or carbon paper. The pressure will transfer the coloured carbon onto the fabric.

LUCKY CHARMS
(Motifs actual size)
P. 136

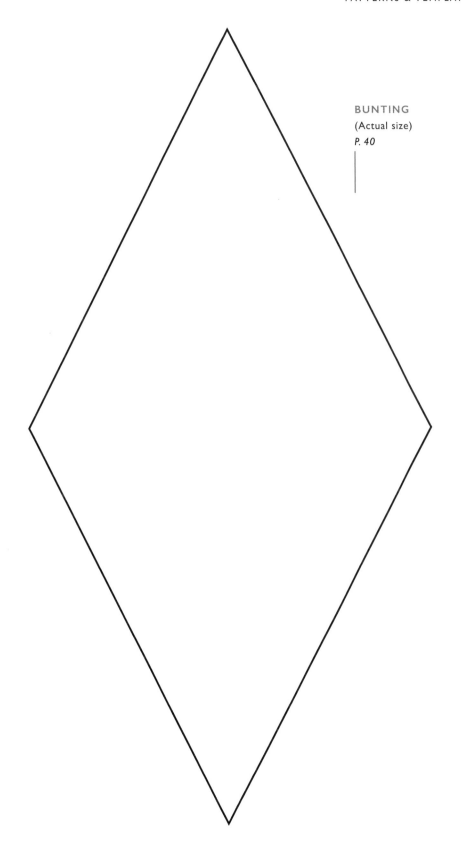

BUNTING
(Actual size)
P. 40

MILESTONE CARDS
(Actual size)
P. 42

MONTH

MONTHS

EMBROIDERED CUSHION
AND MILESTONE CARDS
(Enlarge as required)
P. 16 & P. 42

0 1 2 3 4
5 6 7 8 9

EMBROIDERED CUSHION
(Enlarge as required)
P. 16

A B C D E F G H I
J K L M N O P Q R
S T U V W X Y Z

a b c d e f g h i j k l m n
o p q r s t u v w x y z

CAKE TOPPER TEMPLATES
(Motifs actual size)
P. 44

CAKE TOPPER GUIDES
(Motifs actual size)
P. 44

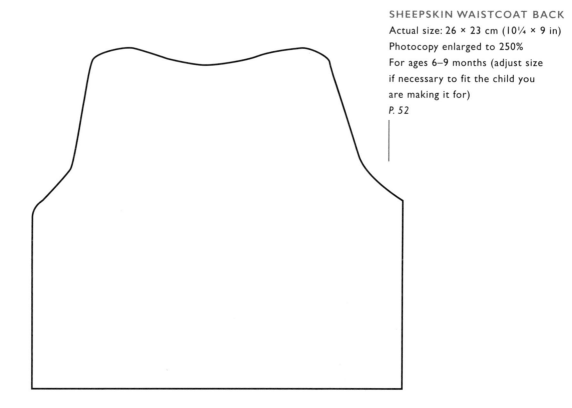

SHEEPSKIN WAISTCOAT BACK
Actual size: 26 × 23 cm (10¼ × 9 in)
Photocopy enlarged to 250%
For ages 6–9 months (adjust size
if necessary to fit the child you
are making it for)
P. 52

SHEEPSKIN WAISTCOAT FRONT
Actual size: 14 × 23 cm (5½ × 9 in)
Photocopy enlarged to 250%
P. 52

LITTLE SAILOR T-SHIRT BACK
Actual size: 32 × 34 cm (12½ × 13¼ in)
Photocopy enlarged to 400%
For ages 6–9 months (adjust size if necessary
to fit the child you are making it for)
P. 72

LITTLE SAILOR T-SHIRT FRONT
Actual size: 32 × 34 cm (12½ × 13¼ in)
Photocopy enlarged to 400%
P. 72

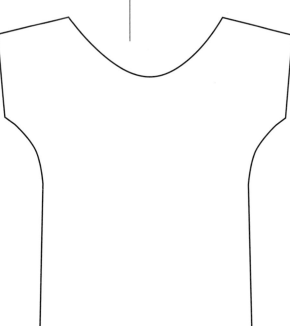

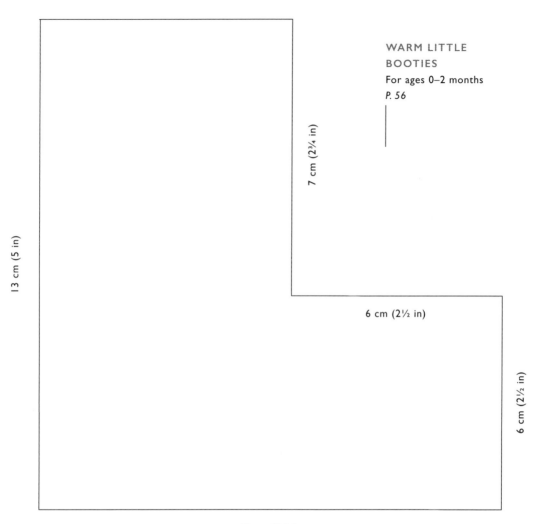

WARM LITTLE
BOOTIES
For ages 0–2 months
P. 56

7 cm (2¾ in)

6 cm (2½ in)

6 cm (2½ in)

13 cm (5 in)

13 cm (5 in)

PERSONALIZED
NAME TAG
P. 64

A B C D E F G H I J K L M N O
P Q R S T U V W X Y Z

BLOOMERS

Actual size: 36 × 23 cm (14 × 9 in)

Photocopy enlarged to 170%

For ages 6–9 months (adjust size if necessary to fit the child you are making it for)

P. 66

FABRIC CROWN
Actual size: 48 × 13 cm
(19 × 5 in)
Photocopy enlarged
to 220%
P. 76

FLUFFY CLOUD MOBILE
(Motifs actual size)
P. 20

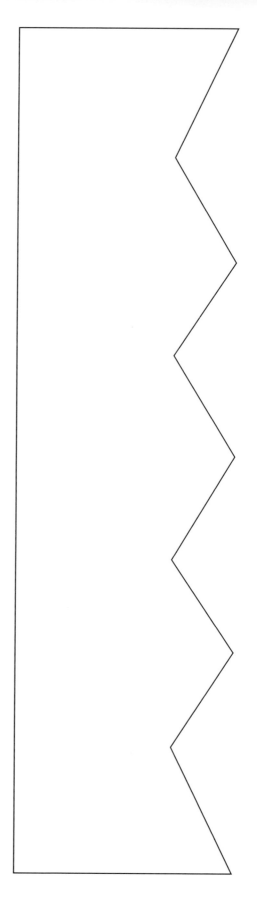

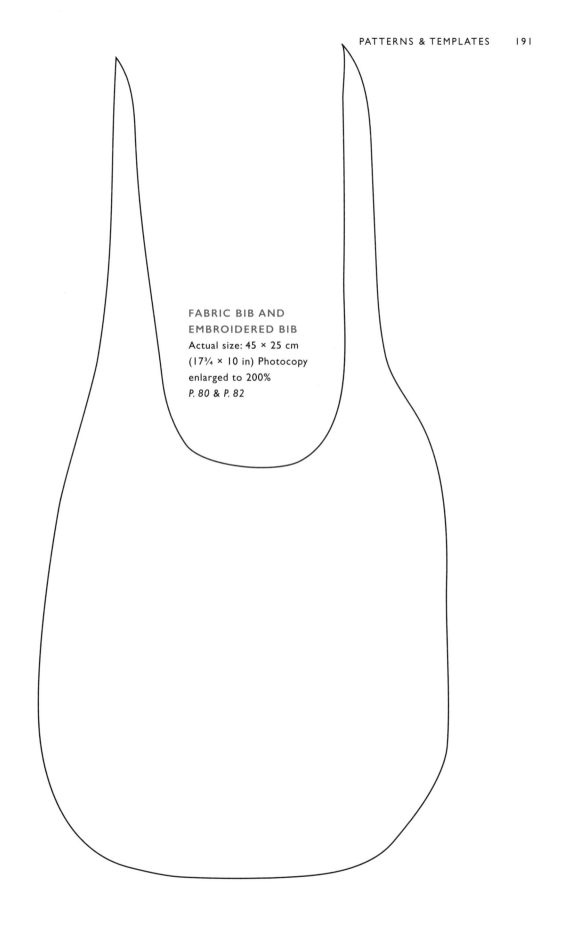

FABRIC BIB AND
EMBROIDERED BIB
Actual size: 45 × 25 cm
(17¾ × 10 in) Photocopy
enlarged to 200%
P. 80 & P. 82

EMBROIDERED BIB
(Actual size)
P. 82

EMBROIDERED BIB
(Actual size)
P. 82

NAPPY POUCH BACK
Actual size: 43 × 20 cm (17 × 8 in)
Photocopy enlarged to 260%
P. 90

NAPPY POUCH FRONT
Actual size: 32 × 20 cm (12½ × 8 in)
Photocopy enlarged to 260%
P. 90

TEXTURED PLAY MAT
(Actual size)
P. 92

CUDDLY LLAMA
Actual size: 27 × 21 cm
(10½ × 8¼ in) Photocopy
enlarged to 190%
P. 110

MINI FINGER PUPPETS
(Motifs actual size)
P. 114

CRIB GARLAND
(Motifs actual size)
P. 146

SOFT CLOUD RATTLE

Actual size: 17 × 11 cm (6½ × 4¼ in)
Photocopy enlarged to 150%
P. 116

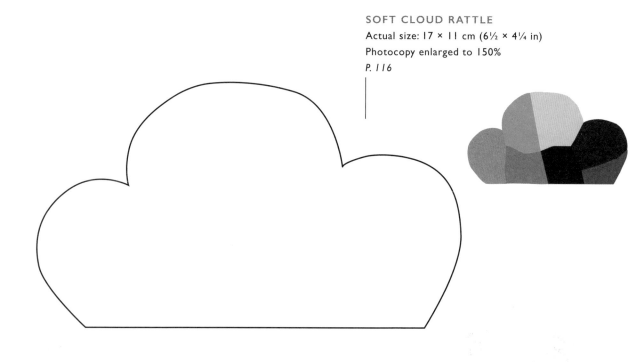

SOFT CLOUD RATTLE – RAINBOW VERSION

Actual size: 17 × 11 cm (6½ × 4¼ in)
Photocopy enlarged to 150%
P. 116

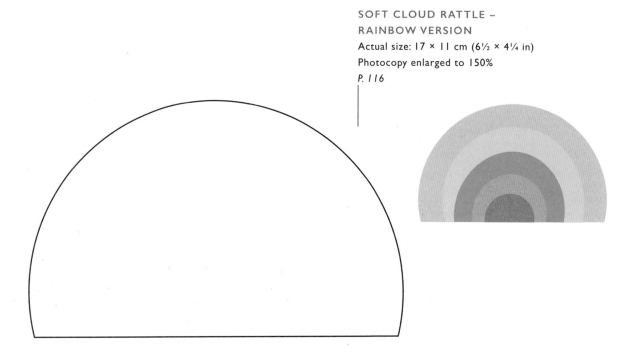

GEOMETRIC MOBILE
Photocopy enlarged
to 200%
P. 124

**COLOUR GUIDE FOR THE
PUNCH NEEDLE CUSHION**
P. 28

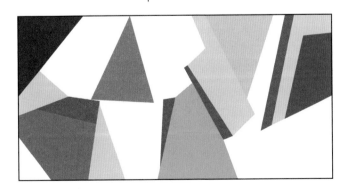

RAINBOW SOFT TOY
Actual size: 28 × 15 cm (11 × 6 in)
Photocopy enlarged to 180%
P. 128

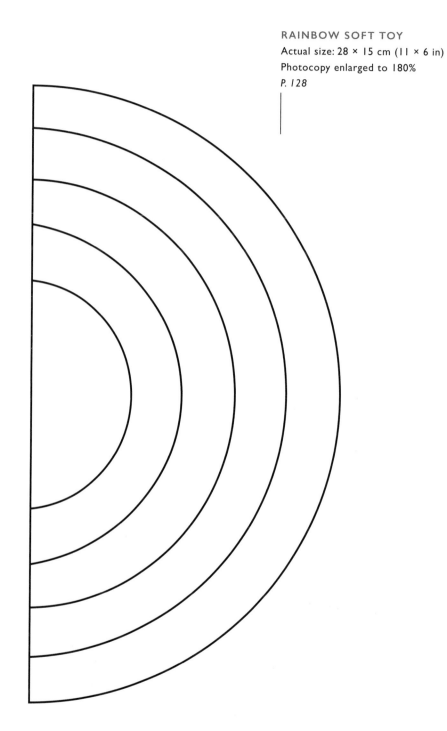

LITTLE TEDDY BEAR
Actual size: 24 × 17 cm (9½ × 6¾ in)
Photocopy enlarged to 210%
P. 132

TEDDY BEAR
WALL HANGING
(Actual size)
P. 22

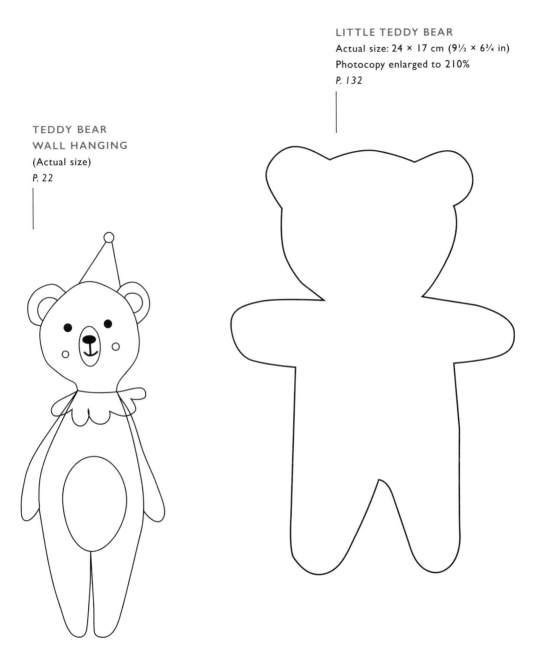

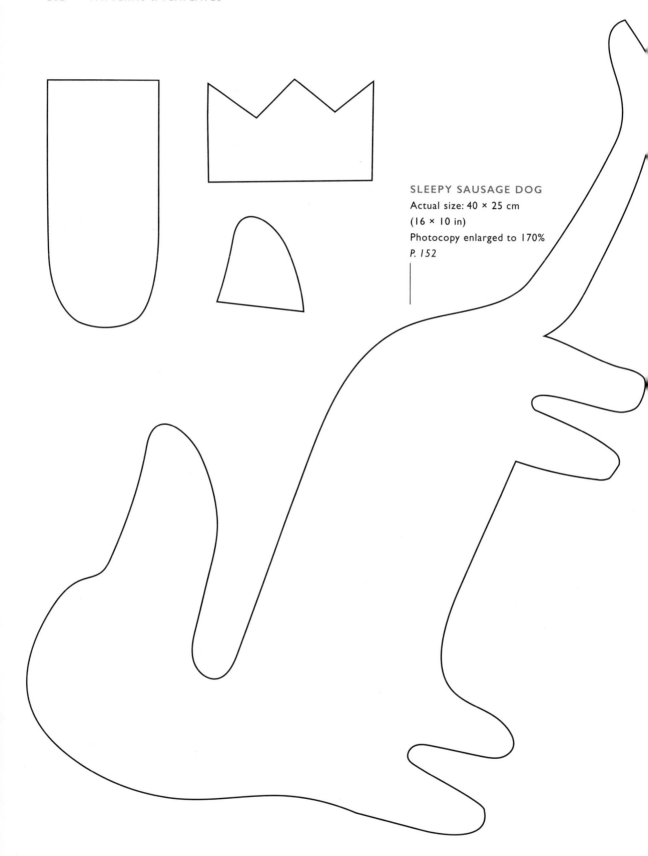

SLEEPY SAUSAGE DOG
Actual size: 40 × 25 cm
(16 × 10 in)
Photocopy enlarged to 170%
P. 152

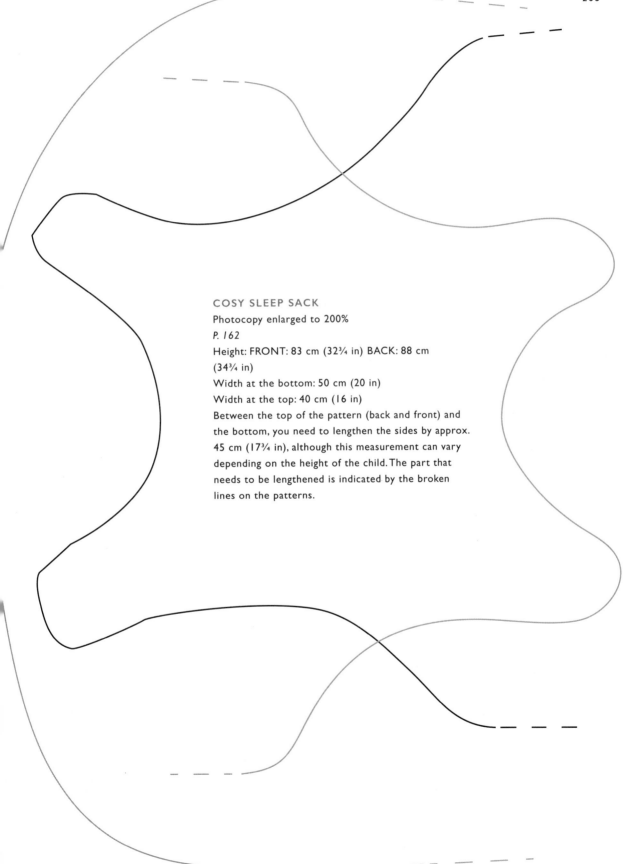

COSY SLEEP SACK
Photocopy enlarged to 200%
P. 162
Height: FRONT: 83 cm (32¾ in) BACK: 88 cm
(34¾ in)
Width at the bottom: 50 cm (20 in)
Width at the top: 40 cm (16 in)
Between the top of the pattern (back and front) and
the bottom, you need to lengthen the sides by approx.
45 cm (17¾ in), although this measurement can vary
depending on the height of the child. The part that
needs to be lengthened is indicated by the broken
lines on the patterns.

CUDDLY LION
BLANKET
(Actual size)
P. 168

INDEX

ACKNOWLEDGEMENTS

My dearest Louise, maybe one day you'll read these words. Thank you for taking part in this adventure – with your little smile that I love so much. You are a wonderful little girl and I could never have dreamed of anyone better than you. I am fulfilled as a mum thanks to you. Mum, thank you for all your help! You helped me make things, move forward, create new memories. You pushed me to work harder and better. Thank you for your advice – and your dressmaker's talent. Julien is always by my side, on every book. This time, as a dad, it made even more sense.

Pascale...yet another book to add to our list of lovely projects, thanks to you. Thank you for having been so kind (and patient!) with me for many months on end. I'm extremely proud of this book, and count myself lucky that our paths crossed a few years ago. Lucile, thank you, my dear Lucile, for your fine scissors and your enthusiasm! It was such a pleasure to be able to work on a project with you. Thank you for your good humour in this whirlwind.

Bérengère and David, thanks a million for Léonie's pretty things, which have taken their rightful place in this book. Marie, thank you for the reel of gold thread, which was a great help! Amélie and Christophe, thank you for allowing me to put my creations in Pablo's lovely bedroom. As with the first book, you've been my lucky star. Annabelle and France, thank you for your respective talents and your gift for beautiful things. Your fabrics were an inspiration. Charline and the DMC team for their wonderful yarns, whose palette of colours is an invitation to be creative.

Amélie, Bérengère, Clélia, Cécile, Émilie, Maïwenn, Virginie, thank you for your daily encouragement, your opinions, and your help. You are precious friends.

Dominique and Frédéric, thank you for having been, once again, my guardian angels – from first draft to proofreading.